FOIL, SABER, AND ÉPÉE FENCING

Maxwell R. Garret
Emmanuil G. Kaidanov
Gil A. Pezza

FOIL, SABER, AND ÉPÉE FENCING

Skills, Safety, Operations, and Responsibilities

The Pennsylvania State University Press
University Park, Pennsylvania

Library of Congress Cataloging-in-Publication Data

Garret, Maxwell R.
    Foil, saber, and épée fencing : skills, safety, operations, and
responsibilities / Maxwell R. Garret, Emmanuil G. Kaidanov,
Gil A. Pezza.

        p.   cm.
    Includes bibliographical references (p.   ) and index.
    ISBN 0-271-01019-3 (alk. paper)
    1. Fencing.   I. Kaidanov, Emmanuil G. II. Pezza, Gil A.
III. Title.
GV1147.G36   1994
796.8'6—dc20   93–17603
                                                                CIP

Published by The Pennsylvania State University Press, Suite C, Barbara Building,
University Park, PA 16802-1003

It is the policy of The Pennsylvania State University Press to use acid-free paper for
the first printing of all clothbound books. Publications on uncoated stock satisfy the
minimum requirements of American National Standard for Information Sciences—
Permanence of Paper for Printed Library Materials, ANSI Z39.48–1984.

Contents

Foreword
by Miguel A. de Capriles

This book is a valuable addition to the growing body of literature in the United States on the sport of fencing. While fencing is one of the most rewarding sports for the participant, it is also one of the least well known in the United States. This book will help to disseminate basic knowledge of the game to all interested persons.

Fencing is practiced formally in about seventy countries that hold active memberships in the Fédération Internationale d'Escrime. The heartland of the fencing world has always been the continent of Europe; the countries of the Americas and of Asia and Africa have generally followed the lead of Europeans in the development of the sport. The current trend toward popularization of this ancient and aristocratic game in all segments of society in the United States was foreshadowed by earlier and similar movements in France, Italy, and Hungary following the First World War and by the strong impetus given to fencing as a "people's sport" on a national scale in the Soviet Union and other East European countries after the Second World War.

Fencing is both old and new. Its infinite variety gives it the capacity for periodic rejuvenation with changing times. At the turn of the twentieth century, the dominant interest of fencers centered upon the endless combinations and permutations of attack and defense that make fencing so similar to chess. Although child prodigies in fencing were not unknown, preeminence in the sport belonged to adults. Today there is a worldwide movement toward simplification of the game, particularly at the competitive level, by concentrating upon a limited number of basic actions, perfectly executed, and on athletic fundamentals—mobility, timing, speed, and endurance. Modern technology has accelerated the process through the electrical judging of touches. This is a game for young people, and young competitors are coming to the fore in fencing as they have done generally in other sports.

In writing this book, the authors have combined their talent and expertise as fencing masters with their experience in the wider field of physical education. Although an earlier book focused on just one weapon—the foil—this book provides technical instruction for all three weapons used by both men and women in competition. Realizing that in this sport there is no real equivalent to the weekend golfer or tennis player, and that some form of organized competition generally provides the greatest satisfaction, even for the fencer who does not aspire to national or international recognition, the authors have wisely included informative chapters on judging and the organization of fencing tournaments, which require the active participation of fencers at all levels of skill.

I want to add a few words of special praise for the sections on safety and legal responsibility—topics that are of enormous importance to fencers, coaches, administrators, and anyone else seriously interested in the healthy development of the sport in the United States.

I congratulate the authors and the publisher of this book.

Miguel A. de Capriles
Former President
Fédération Internationale d'Escrime

Foreword
by Vladimir O. Nazlimov

The first time I met Emmanuil Kaidanov was about thirty years ago. We were both attending the USSR National Squad (Top 24) Saber Tournament in Kharkov, where he grew up and became a well-known and accomplished fencer. Since that time many changes have taken place in the fencing world.

Modern fencers are great athletes. Their physical conditioning must allow them to maintain a high level of performance in a highly intense, competitive environment over extended periods of time—sometimes eight to ten hours a day over three to four days. Many years are needed to develop the specific coordination required to properly perform fencing actions. After reading this book, my feelings returned to the days of my youth in training camps where Emmanuil and I would be required to practice technical actions endlessly in drills. Of course, our young hearts would cry out to start a real fight. In those days a strict reprimand from our coach would cool us off. Only much later did I realize that the foundation for our future victories was laid in the camps with those drills.

While this book is an excellent manual for fencers of all ages, it is particularly appropriate for the young, developing, junior fencer. Coaches whose primary interest is in teaching at the beginner-to-intermediate level should take note of the methodology presented in this work. The drills located in the "Learning Experience" sections are outstanding material for lessons and partner exercises. They are representative of the "classical" formation that Emmanuil Kaidanov and I experienced in our early days. This book is therefore a confident guide, a sure gateway to the wonderful world that can be found in fencing combat: a demanding environment in which one must constantly strive for physical perfection, and where one may find romanticism, courage, and the way of the courteous and considerate person.

I grew up in Dagestan, the mountain country in the Northern Caucasus. The folk wisdom of my people says: A man must complete three tasks in his life: (1) build a house as a foundation for a family; (2) have a son to continue the family line; and (3) grow a tree. In writing this book, Emmanuil Kaidanov and his co-authors grow their trees. This book brings fencing knowledge to the next generation of athletes.

Vladimir O. Nazlimov
World and Olympic Champion
Coach of World Champions

Preface

Since *Foil Fencing* by Maxwell R. Garret and Mary H. Poulson was published in 1981, the fencing movement has rapidly advanced technologically not only in the United States but also worldwide. While the philosophy and principles of participation remain basically the same, the conditions, techniques, equipment, and rules have changed with the times. The present book is a text in the study of all three weapons: foil, saber, and épée. Maxwell Garret, principal author on "Foil," Emmanuil Kaidanov on "Saber," and Gil Pezza on "Épée" have recognized these changes and provided information that will be helpful to the reader. Although the wealth of new material included here is applicable to the immediate present, it has also been weighed with an eye on the future.

The main purpose of this book is to introduce the novice fencer to the game of fencing. It is also intended to share the fun and excitement of fencing with anyone interested, to satisfy a layperson's curiosity regarding the sport of fencing, to help instructors and coaches organize lesson plans, to complement and supplement the fencing instructor's lessons, to assist the experienced fencer in developing the total game, and to inform and guide fencers, coaches/instructors, officials, and administrators regarding safety and legal responsibilities in fencing.

The scope is comprehensive but not exhaustive. This book offers an approach to fencing in which subject matter is structured around concepts. When specifics are forgotten, an understanding of the concept will enable a fencer to recall and apply information more easily. "Learning Experiences" built around these concepts help the fencer learn by doing and, along with the "Highlights" for each chapter, can be easily adapted to fencing lessons.

The authors are grateful to Stephen Sobel, former counsel and current president of the USFA, for contributing the chapter titled "Liability and Negligence."

The authors are deeply indebted to Vladimir O. Nazlimov for his Foreword to this book; to the late Miguel A. de Capriles, whose Foreword to the 1981 book, *Foil Fencing*, is reprinted here with minor changes; and to Mary H. Poulson, for her contributions to the section on foil fencing. They are also indebted to Diana Garret, for acting as sounding board and critic and for providing helpful analytical comments and suggestions; to Esther Garret Solar, for her drawings; to David Shelly, for his professional photographic work; and to Penn State fencers Catherine Kowalski, David Cox, and Geoffrey Russell, for their pictorial contributions; to the United States

Fencing Coaches Association for permission to use excerpts from the USFCA Manual; and to the staff of The Pennsylvania State University Press.

Chapter 3 of this book, "Saber," was prepared with a great deal of participation from Maestro Michael D'Asaro and the kindly advice of A. Jack Keane, Major David Ling, and Maxwell and Diana Garret. A large portion of the material in this chapter has been used in the teaching of the saber course at the USFA Coaches College in Colorado Springs, Colorado.

Above all, the authors hope that each reader will find as much enjoyment and excitement in fencing as the authors themselves have experienced.

Maxwell R. Garret
Emmanuil G. Kaidanov
Gil A. Pezza

1

Introduction

HISTORICAL AND MODERN FENCING

Understanding the history of fencing helps one to develop a deeper appreciation for the sport. The evolution of the sword has been part and parcel of the rise and spread of civilization throughout the world. During prehistoric times, people had to create ways to defend themselves from predators and other humans, and even to conquer them; cavemen first fashioned clubs and then stone axes for these purposes, and from these primitive beginnings more sophisticated weapons were developed. With the advent of Greek and Roman civilization came the invention of short swords, spears, and shields. In modern times, the sword has become more a sporting weapon than a weapon of war or an implement for survival.

The Importance of the Sword in the History of Civilization

The earliest recorded evidence of a practice fencing bout or tournament is found in a relief carving in the temple of Madinat Habu, near Luxor in Upper Egypt, built by Rameses III about 1190 B.C. The fencers are shown wearing masks, their weapon points covered, with narrow shields for parrying strapped to their rear arms. Spectators and officials appear in the background.

The history of the sword, however, begins much earlier—indeed, before written history. From the advent of metal weapons in the Bronze Age, swords were fashioned in many forms. The copper dagger used in the Aegean region was succeeded by a longer weapon called the dirk, which eventually was transformed into the sword.

Swords in the Middle Ages were heavy and clumsy. For many years the two-handed sword was used in combat, heavy armor playing an important defensive role. The styles of fighting were primitive; the strongest arm and the heaviest weapon usually prevailed. When gunpowder was introduced in the fourteenth century, heavy armor became impractical. Many changes in tactics and weapons quickly followed, and swords were transformed into lighter, more manageable weapons.

The Development of Tactical Skills

Before 1500, swords were primarily slashing/cutting weapons. After 1500, lighter thrusting weapons, such as the one-handed rapier, became popular and part of a gentleman's attire. The rapier was used chiefly for attack; defense was entrusted to the rear hand, which carried a dagger, cloak, or buckler.

Guilds of fencing masters developed throughout Europe to impart the skills of swordsmanship. Each guild or fencing school guarded its tactics and programs from competitors. The various guilds and schools developed new fencing techniques. Footwork based on geometric designs was formulated by the Spanish fencing masters. The lunge came into being in the latter half of the sixteenth century. The creation of a single weapon effective for both attack and defense led to the modern fencing positions, which provide a minimum target area to the opponent and give the fencer a longer-reaching lunge.

Italian masters in the seventeenth century furthered the development of fencing with the riposte, an attacking movement that immediately follows a parry. Other refinements included the introduction of the French foil around 1650, the evolution of the duelling sword in the sixteenth and seventeenth centuries, and the development of the fencing mask for practice by La Boissiere, an eighteenth-century French fencing master who helped students learn to fence safely.

Proficiency in the art of fencing became an important skill and a necessary accomplishment for the nobility and many other members of the leisure class.

The Significance of Duelling and Duelling Weapons

With the growth of duelling during the sixteenth and seventeenth centuries, the rapier was replaced by the colichemarde, a thin-bladed weapon that eventually gave way to the small French court sword. The outcome of a duel during this era was considered an expression of God's will, and so the duel was a means for settling disputes. It was not uncommon for armorers and swordsmiths to carve into the blades quotations such as "Trust in God and Me," "Do Not Draw Me Without Reason," "Do Not Sheathe Me Without Honor," and "Saint Simon Is My Guide."

Faith in divine approval of the outcome characterized many trials in battle and furthered the chivalric tradition of the Middle Ages. Later the duel was used to settle legal claims and disputes regarding personal honor. In fact, so many were killed as a result of these encounters that duelling was banned in France and England. However, the edict did little to prevent these personal conflicts.

About the middle of the seventeenth century, the Italian school developed the "firetta"; the French, the "fleuret"; and the English, the "foil." The foil, which has a slender, tapered quadrangular blade with a small bell guard, became the training weapon for duelling. The duelling weapon had a triangular blade, similar to the épée used today. Consequently, the foil is considered the basic weapon for those who want to master the épée.

The duel had great impact on fencing as a sport, providing the traditions of courtesy, customs, officiating, and tactics.

French and Italian Influence on Fencing

The rivalry between the French and Italian schools gave rise to the first international tournaments. Fencing masters from both France and Italy migrated to England, Germany, and other countries, where they were well received. In England, King Henry VIII welcomed them and gave his blessing to the sport of fencing, which became a national pastime during the sixteenth, seventeenth, and eighteenth centuries. The French and Italian schools reigned supreme during the seventeenth century. By the beginning of the nineteenth century, fencing had developed into a sport with its own rules.

The Progression to Modern Fencing

In the nineteenth century the saber was accepted as the national weapon of Hungary. The French school developed the foil and the épée, which with slight modifications are the weapons used in competition today. Weapons gradually became lighter and better balanced, resulting in a sport that emphasizes speed of blade and body.

With these developments, the outlawing of duelling except as a sport, and the creation of the modern Olympic Games in 1896 in Athens, Greece, fencing developed into a popular activity. In the last century and a half, the sword has not generally been worn except for military and ceremonial occasions.

People may have forgotten the role and impact of the sword on history, but its influence on dress and custom persists. Buttons on the backs of dress coats exist because they once supported a sword belt. Ladies take a gentleman's left arm, for in earlier times gentlemen wanted the right arm free for drawing the sword. And men's coats are buttoned toward the right for ease in opening them with the left hand as the right hand reached for the sword.

Fencing terminology is extensive and quite different from that used in other sports. Many of the terms are of French derivation—in fact, the official language for fencing is French.

FENCING ORGANIZATIONS

Fencing is organized under national and international governing federations. The United States Fencing Association (USFA), previously known as the Amateur Fencing League of America (AFLA), was founded in 1891 by twenty enthusiasts. The National Fencing Coaches Association of America (NFCAA), known today as the United States Fencing Coaches Association (USFCA), was chartered in 1941. Both organizations have promoted interest and participation in fencing among individuals and institutions.

The United States Fencing Association (USFA)

The USFA is the official governing body for amateur fencing in the United States and is so recognized by the Fédération Internationale d'Escrime and the United States Olympic Committee. The USFA cooperates with the National Collegiate Athletic Association and the United States Fencing Coaches Association. For further information on fencing in the United States, contact:

> USFA National Headquarters
> One Olympic Plaza
> Colorado Springs, CO 80909-5774
> Telephone: (719) 578-4511

The United States Fencing Coaches Association (USFCA)

Many of the United States fencing coaches are members of the USFCA. It is the first coaches' association to have developed an accreditation program that examines candidates for certification as Instructor, Prevost, and Master.

The United States National Academy of Arms

The International Academy of Arms, headquartered in Paris, France, is the governing body for all twenty-six National Fencing Academies. The United States Fencing Coaches Association is the prevailing arm, known as the United States National Academy of Arms, established in March 1974. Accredited fencing masters, prevosts, and instructors—all of whom belong to the USFCA, which administers the accreditation program—are entitled to membership in the National Academy. As stated in the USFCA bylaws, this group "resolves to improve, promote and foster the highest quality of fencing and the highest ideals of sportsmanship in competitions with fencing masters all over the world, through defining and establishing the criteria of fencing education in colleges, through setting standards for teaching accreditation, and through acting as an advisory body to amateur groups and associations."

Representing the USFCA to the International Academy of Arms is Vice-President Jean-Jacques Gillet. For further information about the National Academy, contact:

United States Fencing Coaches Association
P.O. Box 274
New York, NY 10159
Telephone: (212) 532-2557

SOURCES OF FENCING INSTRUCTION

Fencing has attracted such a large number of enthusiasts that there are active fencing groups in most metropolitan areas and in many smaller cities and towns in the United States. To locate a fencing group, check with local groups, such as the Young Men's and Women's Christian Associations (YMCAs or YWCAs) and Young Men's and Women's Hebrew Associations (YMHAs or YWHAs), community center, recreation department, high school, or college or university, or write to the USFA or USFCA headquarters. If there is no fencing group in your community, one can be organized and sponsored through an established institution.

LEARNING EXPERIENCE—FENCING HISTORY AND ORGANIZATIONS

1. *Visit a museum or antique shop and examine the various types of swords and armor used in the past. Compare them with present-day fencing equipment. Note the changes in style, shape, and weight.*
2. *Watch a historical movie that includes sword fighting and compare that with a modern fencing bout. Are the styles historically authentic? List the differences observed.*
3. *Locate copies of the official constitution and bylaws of the USFA and USFCA. Describe the differences between the two.*

HIGHLIGHTS

1. List several historical events in the development of modern fencing.
2. Name the governing bodies of fencing in the United States and explain the function of each.
3. Name the local fencing group(s). If none exists, how would you start one?

THE ATTRACTION OF FENCING

Fencing is a fine combative sport that provides lifetime opportunities for participation and creative expression. Cyrano de Bergerac, D'Artagnan, the Three Musketeers—

who has not dreamed of walking side by side with these swordsmen, confident of being able to handle any situation, of being the master of one's own fate? This need not be an idle dream. Learning to fence is within anyone's grasp.

Many Opportunities for Participation

Fencing is a year-round sport with many attractive attributes. It can be conducted either indoors or outdoors on a nonskid surface; boys and girls as well as men and women can enjoy the sport; people of any age, body build, or temperament can experience success; and a fencing practice area may be as small as a living room or as large as all outdoors.

Many high schools, colleges, voluntary and public agencies, and private clubs provide facilities and fencing instruction not only throughout the United States but also all over the world. From their interest and participation in fencing, many people have developed hobbies, such as collecting weapons, books, fencing manuscripts, duelling prints, and art objects pertaining to the sport.

Variety of Fencing Competitions

Opportunities for fencing competition are almost endless. There are local and divisional tournaments open to anyone interested. Sectional, national, and international tournaments are conducted for those who qualify from the local and divisional events. The Junior Olympic fencing program provides age groupings for Under-17 and Under-20 and sponsors an annual national championship from which fencers are selected to represent the United States at the Cadet and Junior World Championships. USFA tournaments are held for novices, teams, and individuals according to their classifications, including senior-age fencers—those over forty. The ultimate in fencing competition is to be selected to represent one's country in the Olympics, the Pan American Games, the World Fencing Championships, or the World University Games.

The Satisfactions of Fencing

Once their interest is captured, people pursue fencing for the same reasons they pursue many other activities, such as singing, painting, playing musical instruments, solving mathematical problems, piloting airplanes or boats, or playing basketball. These activities satisfy their need to use their abilities as significant, creative, self-reliant, and confident beings.

LEARNING EXPERIENCE—THE ATTRACTION OF FENCING

Why are you attracted to fencing? When you think of fencing, what images come to mind?

Many lessons of life can be learned on the fencing strip. Fencing provides opportunities to reduce tensions and increase satisfactions, and it helps develop discipline and self-confidence. It also teaches and demonstrates that—

Hard work can be satisfying.
Exercise is important for total fitness.
One can be defeated and then bounce back to victory.
Failure is merely a detour to success.
Aggressive feelings can be channeled into higher emotional attitudes.
In confronting many problem situations, one can learn to come up with solutions.

Paul Gallico, a well-known author and columnist who began fencing at age thirty-seven, spoke from experience about the attraction of fencing:

> [It is the] release trigger for the outpouring of personality, temperament and self. It is an axiom of fencing that five minutes on a strip behind a weapon,

and a fencer has revealed himself, his nature, his character, his honesty, his mental capacities—his very essence. As you are, so you will fence. You can conceal nothing, nor can your opponent. Your inner selves will clash upon the strip as sharply as your steel—there is no royal road, no easy shortcut to the joys of combat fencing. The price is . . . hard work and discipline, of sometimes tedious practice routines. But the rewards thereof are great and satisfying. Once the drudgery has been put behind, the fun comes fast and furious and never ending.*

Fencing promotes physical, emotional, and mental growth. Fencers depend on their ability, ingenuity, comprehension, judgment, and skill, with no assistance from outside sources. Unlike some team games, no substitute player or special play can be introduced into the bout.

Many competitions are held on round-robin schedules, and it is not unusual for a fencer in a national tournament to fence fifteen to twenty-five bouts in a day. Such a schedule places a premium on endurance and requires skill, agility, balance, quickness, power, and good coordination.

To cross blades with an opponent requires courage. Even though the weapons are blunted and flexible, and even though all safety precautions have been taken, a beginner may feel shy and reluctant to be touched by a weapon. But courage can be developed and instilled. The development of courage can be of great psychological value to the fencer, enhancing self-confidence and the ability to make decisions under stress.

LEARNING EXPERIENCE—LESSONS OF LIFE

Take special note of the lessons of life that can be learned in fencing. When you have entered your first competition after acquiring the basic skills, check the list again to see which lessons you have learned on the strip.

WEAPONS, THE TARGET, AND THE FIELD OF PLAY

The essence of fencing is touching and not being touched by one's opponent. Fencers use the weapon as the tool.

Fencers must acquire a delicate sense of touch and instantaneous response using trigger-fast reflexive movements as well as skillful deception. Success in this sport depends on such personal qualities as intelligence, power of observation, mental control, strategy, coordination, dexterity, and agility. Leg strength, height, and length of reach are also factors that determine progress in any of the weapons.

*Quoted in Aldo Nadi, *On Fencing* (New York: G. P. Putnam's Sons, 1943), p. xv.

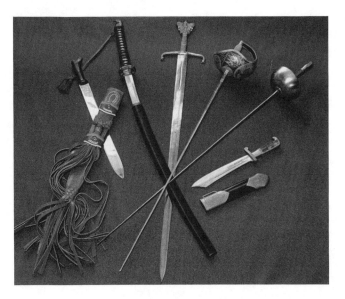

The Weapons

Three weapons are used in the sport of fencing: foil, saber, and épée.

   While the target area and the style of fencing differ according to the weapon, there are similarities in technique and timing. Most fencers begin their training in foil, progressing to saber or épée. Some concentrate on developing proficiency in one weapon, others become proficient in two weapons, and some in three. Because many skills learned in foil generally apply to saber and épée, the first section of this book deals with foil fencing. In foil fencing, a beginner learns skills that apply to all three weapons.

Differences Among Foil, Épée, Saber

Weapon	Target	Method of Scoring	Blade Description	Original Use of Weapon
Foil	Torso	With tip only	Slender, tapered quadrangular blade; small bell guard	Training
Épée	Entire body	With tip only	Thick, tapered triangular blade; large, heavy bell guard	Duelling
Saber	Entire body above the hip line	With tip and cutting edge	Y- or T-shaped; large, crescent-shaped bell guard	Cavalry

LEARNING EXPERIENCE—FOIL, ÉPÉE, SABER

1. *Ask a fencer to show you the three basic weapons and to explain their similarities and differences.*
2. *Observe competition in foil, épée, and saber, noting especially the similarities in technique and timing and the differences in target areas and styles.*

The Target

Fencing is a combat sport, the object of which is to hit the opponent on the target with the point of the weapon, and also by a cutting action in saber.

The valid target in foil fencing includes the trunk of the body from the collar to the groin in front and to a horizontal line passing across the top of the hip bones on the back—that is, the area outlined by a metallic jacket, shown below. The arms, legs, mask, and the bib of the mask are not valid target areas. A graze or slap with the weapon is not a valid hit.

In saber fencing, the valid target includes the head, arms, and upper body above the hip line. There is no off-target or invalid hit. If a fencer touches an invalid surface, it is considered as if one missed the target.

In épée fencing, the entire body is valid target. The fencer can score by touching any part of the opponent's body: the head, the toe, the trunk, etc.

Foil Target

Saber Target

Épeé Target

Valid Target Areas Shown in White

The Field of Play

A fencing bout is conducted on a rectangular strip (piste or mat) that has the layout and dimensions in the accompanying diagram showing the regulation strip for all three weapons. A fencer wins the bout by scoring five valid hits or touches on the opponent. The time limit for scoring five touches is four minutes of actual fencing time.

HIGHLIGHTS

1. Explain the similarities and differences among the three fencing weapons.
2. Point out the limits of the valid target.
3. Describe the differences between a valid hit and an invalid hit.
4. Identify and name the main areas of a fencing strip.
5. State the time limit and the number of hits required for winning a bout.
6. List several physical, mental, and emotional values to be gained from fencing.

THE FENCER'S GEAR

For all three weapons, certain basic equipment is needed: weapon, glove, jacket (including protective plastron and breast protectors for women), mask, knickers, and shoes and socks.

The Weapon

A good weapon for the fencer is the same as a good violin for the musician. Knowing how to select, care for, and maintain the equipment is imperative. Information regarding special gear for each of the three weapons is in Chapters 2, 3, and 4. The standard weapon is composed of blade, bell guard, pad, handle, and pommel. A new weapon will arrive assembled unless otherwise requested. The *blade* is tapered to a blunted tip. The *pommel* is attached to the threaded end of the blade. The *foible* of the blade is the part near the tip that is thinnest and weakest. The area closest to the *bell guard* is the strong part, or *forté*.

A blade may be no longer than 90 centimeters for foil and épée, and no longer

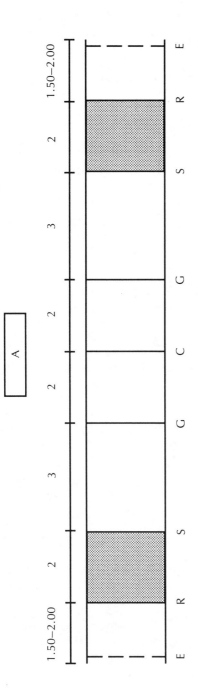

A

1.50–2.00 2 3 2 2 3 2 1.50–2.00

E R S G C G S R E

A = Table for electrical apparatus   C = Center line

G = On-guard lines   S = Start of 2-meter signal area

E = End of strip extensions   R = Rear limit of strip

For electrical weapons, the metallic strip must cover the entire length and breadth of the strip, including the extensions.

Note: All dimensions are given in meters.

Regulation Strip for All Three Weapons

than 88 centimeters for saber. Up to this limit, blade length may vary. While a shorter blade does not reach as far, some believe it has less whip and therefore can be better controlled.

The Foil

Blades are currently manufactured in France, Poland, Italy, England, the Ukraine, Hungary, and China. Blades can be x-rayed to uncover weak spots in the steel. Consult experienced fencers or instructors about what brand of blade is the most durable and will give the best service.

The "maraging" blades have recently been gaining in popularity, and they are mandatory for foil and épée in international competitions. These blades are more expensive, but their long life expectancy makes them an attractive buy.

Though flexible, new blades are very straight. It is essential that a new blade be bent so that the point deviates downward. This bend will increase blade life by causing it always to bend in the same direction. The bending of the blade ensures the safety of a fencer by absorbing the force of the impact when the blade touches the target.

LEARNING EXPERIENCE—BENDING THE BLADE

1. *Examine several used blades. Are they bent properly? Why should they be?*
2. *Practice maintaining the proper bend of the blade: Hold the weapon with the handle close to the floor and slide the sole of the foot along the foible of the blade until a slight downward curve or bend has been set along the forward part of the blade. An experienced fencer or instructor can demonstrate how to bend the blade properly.*

Although the tip of the nonelectrical foil or épée blade is blunted, it is nevertheless steel and requires additional padding by wrapping adhesive tape around the tip or by covering it with rubber or plastic protective tips.

The blade is the only part of the weapon that occasionally needs to be replaced. With care, the remaining parts will give many years of service. Fine sandpaper can remove rough edges or rust that may appear. Extra blades and rubber or plastic tips should be ordered when purchasing a nonelectrical foil or épée.

The guard, or bell guard, made from either steel or aluminum, is a concave plate that protects the hand and arm from the opponent's hits. It is lined with a leather or felt pad that cushions the fingers.

The handle (hilt or grip) is made of wood, plastic, or metal. It may be covered with leather stripping, heavy cord, plastic twine, or insulating material.

Three basic handle shapes for foil and épée were developed from the French, Italian, and Spanish schools of fencing. The French school, which uses a straight handle, stressed fingerplay. The thumb and forefinger served as manipulators of the blade; the other three fingers were used as aids.

The Italians added a crosspiece to the bell guard. The thumb and forefinger gripped the flattened portion (ricasso) of the blade; the middle finger passed through

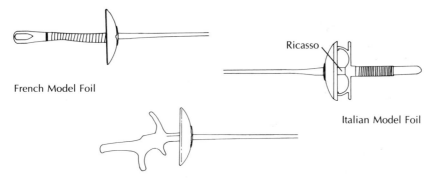

French Model Foil

Ricasso

Italian Model Foil

Belgian Model Foil (orthopedic, or pistol, handle)

Basic Handle Shapes

the outer ring between the guard and the crosspiece; the other two fingers were placed on the handle, which was bound to the wrist by a strap. These factors enabled the fencer to use strong, forceful movements. The Italian school used to emphasize an on-guard position with the blade almost horizontal and the weapon arm almost fully extended.

Handles gripped as a pistol—for example, the Belgian model—received their inspiration from Spanish schools and are classified as orthopedic types. It was believed that they enabled the fencer to use both strength and fingerplay to the best advantage.

Most fencing teachers in the United States recommend that a beginner use a foil or épée with a French handle. It is the least expensive and is widely used. More important, many instructors believe that beginners can best learn the nuances of fingerplay with this type of handle.

The pommel is a metal counterweight that secures the handle, the bell guard, and the blade. Many pommels have a hole at the end into which an eye-screw can be inserted for suspending the foil when it is not in use.

Electrical Weapons

Electrical weapons are currently used in almost all competitions. Most foil and épée fencers today use an orthopedic handle with the electrical weapon. In tournament play, each fencer is required to have at least two operable weapons.

The body cords for the electrical foil and the electrical saber are the same, but the body cord for the épée is different. Like all electrical wires, the body cord should be treated with extreme care and checked frequently to ensure against malfunction.

LEARNING EXPERIENCE—COMPARISON OF VARIETY OF WEAPONS

Examine several different styles of thrusting weapons. Compare quality, style, and price. Which weapon is best for you? Discuss your weapon needs with your instructor/coach or an experienced fencer.

HIGHLIGHTS

1. Identify the parts of a weapon.
2. State the advantages of the short blade and the longer blade.
3. Explain why a new blade should be bent, in what direction, and how it should be done.
4. Describe the tip of the blade and how it should be covered.
5. Explain the purpose of the guard.
6. Identify the three basic handle shapes for thrusting weapons and explain the purpose of each.
7. Explain why the French-style handle is recommended for beginners.
8. State the functions of the pommel.
9. Explain the advantages of using an electrical weapon with an orthopedic handle.

The Glove

A padded glove and gauntlet are essential to protect the fencer from injury. The glove is usually made of suede or other leather and is sometimes reinforced at points that wear out most readily. However, any glove with gauntlet (padded cuff that extends over the sleeve of the jacket) is suitable if it prevents the opponent's weapon from entering the sleeve of the fencer's jacket.

To prevent the glove from being hardened by perspiration, allow it to dry at room temperature after each use. To aid the drying process, insert absorbent material into the glove. For shape retention, a replica of a hand inside the glove is useful. A few drops of neat's-foot oil will keep the glove soft and pliable. To extend the life of a glove, reinforce the areas where the handle comes in contact with the glove.

The Jacket

A safe fencing jacket is one that provides sufficient protection and padding. The fencing jacket should fit snugly but not too tightly. According to the rules of the USFA, all women's jackets must have extra protection in the bust area. In addition, the wearing of a plastron (a padded garment with one sleeve) is obligatory for both men and women to ensure added protection of the target area. Since the groin area is a valid target, it is mandatory that a jacket with a cuissard (groin strap) be worn. In electrical foil fencing, the fencer must wear a lamé (metallic jacket) over the fencing jacket covering the valid target.

Front jacket closings must have the open edge directed away from the foil arm.

The lower edge of the jacket must overlap the knickers by at least 10 centimeters (4 inches) when the fencer is in the on-guard position.

Repair any holes or worn spots immediately, and wash jackets often. To avoid shrinkage, follow the manufacturer's instructions, or wash in lukewarm water, rinse, and always hang to dry. Bleach weakens cloth fibers. Use it sparingly if at all.

A loose-fitting jacket offers a larger target, so select a jacket that is form-fitting but still allows freedom of movement. A cotton T-shirt worn underneath the jacket will absorb perspiration as well as give added protection.

A fencer whose hair touches the jacket needs to pin it up so that it cannot become entwined around a blade or invalidate a touch or hit made on the metallic vest.

The Mask

Safety considerations require that a mask be well constructed, free of dents, and fit the head snugly. The bib should cover the neck area.

Heavy mesh wiring soldered together for reinforcement is used in the construction of a mask. Dents weaken the mesh. Should denting occur, the mask should be repaired and refurbished, a service that some manufacturers provide. Masks with rusted mesh are dangerous and should be discarded.

Masks may be purchased in different sizes and can be adjusted for safety and comfort. They may be trimmed with canvas, plastic, or leather. The bib of the mask must be heavy white quilted cloth or plastic, permanently attached to the mask. The bib should be cleaned frequently.

According to the USFA and FIE rules, "The mesh of the mask, both at the front and at the sides, must be able to withstand, without permanent deformation, the introduction into the mesh of a conical instrument (the angle of the surface of the cone being at 4 degrees to the axis) at a pressure of 12 kilograms." All masks must be checked at every official competition.

Knickers, Shoes, and Socks

It is necessary to wear fencing knickers to protect the legs. Many fencers wear sweatpants during fencing practice. The USFA recently disallowed use of any other clothing but fencing knickers, in order to protect the legs and groin area. Shorts are definitely unsuitable and unsafe. Knickers and knee socks are required during competitions. For added protection, men should wear athletic supporters.

Shoes must have rubber soles to provide traction and comfort. Never fence in shoes with hard leather soles, in bare feet, or in stocking feet.

SELECTING FENCING GEAR

An experienced fencer or a fencing instructor can help you make your selection. Certain guidelines should be followed when purchasing fencing equipment:

Order equipment early. Order early through an institution or a sporting-goods store, to ensure prompt delivery and to allow time for making adjustments or exchanging equipment. All personal equipment should be marked for identification.

Be properly fitted. The materials used for knickers and jackets should be preshrunk to ensure proper fit. Shoes and socks must fit well to avoid blisters and other foot discomforts. Masks should fit snugly. If eyeglasses are worn, masks should accommodate the glasses without creating an uncomfortable feeling for the fencer.

Purchase high-quality equipment. The mask, jacket, knickers, and glove are necessary protective gear. Do not sacrifice safety by purchasing inferior equipment.

Order from reputable sources known to provide good service and high-quality products. A good representative listing of fencing equipment suppliers may be found in *American Fencing* and *The Swordmaster* publications.

Keep informed of rule changes affecting equipment requirements. Arrange with fencing manufacturers and dealers to receive their latest equipment catalogs. Note changes in design, materials, and protective features.

LEARNING EXPERIENCE—EQUIPMENT COMPARISON

Examine several designs of fencing equipment. Compare quality, style, and prices. Which equipment is best for you? Discuss equipment needs with your instructor or coach or with an experienced fencer.

HIGHLIGHTS

1. State the functions of the glove and how it should be cared for.
2. List three criteria for determining a suitable jacket.
3. Describe a safe, functional mask.
4. Describe how a mask is tested for safety.
5. State the functions of knickers and rubber-soled shoes.
6. List four guidelines for equipment selection.

2

Foil

INTRODUCTION

Most books are written to provide an extraordinary experience for others to enjoy. We strive to do likewise. In a book that covers the fundamentals of training and progresses to the teaching of skills and strategies for all three fencing weapons, a logical sequence of instruction is necessary. The basic instruction in the use of the foil is also applicable for saber and épée.

With the technological advancements of electrical scoring devices, most USFA-sanctioned tournaments require the use of electrical apparatus. Therefore, this book includes information on the use, composition, and care of the electrical weapons.

The training process in this book is designed to help the student master the basic elements of the sport and to continue to improve his or her skills through a series of lesson plans. The authors then provide the fencer and the coach or instructor with strategies to help the fencer develop an analytical approach to the sport. By stressing the importance of practicing against an opponent, the student soon learns the skills necessary for participation in competition. We also want to present the sport of fencing as an activity that can provide a lifetime of enjoyment while rewarding the participant with physical, mental, and social benefits. In life we learn that few things of value come without effort.

THE DEVELOPMENT OF FOIL FENCING

Understanding the development of foil fencing will promote appreciation of the weapon. The first weapon used in organized fencing was the foil. The foil was designed as a practice weapon for people who wanted to become proficient in the duelling sword (the épée).

The European Influence

The French, Italian, Belgian, and Hungarian fencing masters who migrated to the United States in the late nineteenth century and the twentieth century helped tremendously to improve the technique of American fencing enthusiasts. According to sport historians Jeffrey Tishman and Allen Zeyher, the first fencing organization in the United States was the New York Turnverein, which was established in 1850 and which hired General Franz Siegel, a Badenese army officer, as their fencing master in 1851. Subsequently, many distinguished fencing masters—including René Pinchard (former coach at the New York Fencers Club), Joseph Fiems and Clovis Deladrier (former coaches at the U.S. Naval Academy), Robert Grasson (from Belgium, and former coach at Yale University), Joseph Vince (former coach at the City College of New York), Lajos S. Csiszar (former coach at the University of Pennsylvania), Georgio Santelli and Csaba Elthes (from Hungary), and Julio M. Castello from Spain (former coach at Yale University and New York University)—became some of the legendary fencing masters in the United States.

The Three Stages of Development

There are three stages in the development of foil fencing as a sport:

Stage One:
1. The foil created (18th century).
2. Fencing mask designed.
3. Number of fencing masters increases.

Stage Two:
1. Fencing rules established.
2. Amateur Fencers League of America (AFLA) established in 1891. Now known as the United States Fencing Association (USFA).

3. Regional and local fencing governing bodies established, in addition to the national organization (the USFA).
4. The first Olympiad in Athens, Greece, in 1896; the Fédération Internationale d'Escrime (FIE) established.
5. United States Fencing Coaches Association (USFCA) established in 1948.

Stage Three:
1. Electrical weapon(s) and scoring devices introduced in 20th century (with constant development and refinement of weapons and equipment over time).
2. Training and coaching programs developed under the aegis of the USFA and the USFCA.
3. Clinics and workshops begin to be sponsored by local and regional governing bodies, permitting establishment of a nationwide network for improving all aspects of the sport of fencing.

The Effect of Electrical Scoring Apparatus

Until the electrical apparatus was developed and utilized, a director (or president) and four judges did the officiating. ("Director" or "President" has now been replaced by "Referee.") The introduction of electrical foil fencing allowed the director (now referee) to become the only official to determine "right of way," according to pre-scribed conventions of foil play, and to award the score.

The advent of electrical apparatus in the 1950s caused much controversy. It was feared that this new apparatus might cause changes in tactics, technique, style, and officiating—to the detriment of the sport. But the universal acceptance of electrical apparatus was a major factor in the increased interest and revitalization of the sport of foil fencing. With the introduction of electrical foil scoring and recording apparatus, the classical conventions of play were diminished, and more spectacular tactics and techniques were introduced in the struggle to score touches (hits).

American Schools of Instruction

It is difficult to identify any specific national school of instruction in modern-day tournament play. Most contemporary fencers develop their own style, reflecting the teaching of their fencing master, who tends to develop the basic natural qualities of the student while following the standardized instruction skills and techniques de-scribed in this text.

Michael Marx (seven-time winner of the Division One U.S. Men's Foil Championship), takes a personal look at some of the great fencers in the United States:

> As a young competitor, I was awed by the likes of Ed Ballinger, Albie Axelrod, Maxine Mitchell, Paul Pesthy, Marty Lang, Nikki Franke, John Nonna, Alex Orban, Gay D'Asaro, Ed Donofrio, and countless others. As time passed, I

came to know many of these people and soon realized that their greatness came not from their impressive records but from their character.

Some of these great fencers loved winning, others hated losing. Some displayed technical genius, while others were crafty and swift; some would fight for every touch, while another would seem to play. I watched them confound opponents, amaze spectators, and win numerous national titles. I also watched them get soundly beaten during their slow, silent fall from grace. What impressed me most was how human they were. They were just people, not idols or heroes. When they were fencing, their egos took a back seat. They gave what they had—win or lose. If they beat you (though at times it looked too easy), they worked for it. And if you beat them, you earned your victory.

These great athletes seemed able to simplify the incredibly complex sport in which they were competing. The diversity of the sport, combining technique, tactics, and mental and physical attributes, can be mind-boggling. Eighteen years ago, Maître Yves Auriol said six words that simplified the sport in my mind: "The answer is on the strip." These words changed my life. As I started achieving results myself, I experienced many benefits. I traveled to foreign countries, felt the excitement of competing at the Olympic level, and developed lasting friendships while learning about new cultures. At times, it seemed difficult to be friends with individuals who may take my place on the next team, but that is where character comes in. Good luck.

LEARNING EXPERIENCE—FOIL FENCING POPULARITY

Discuss with your instructor and/or senior fencer what foil fencing was like before and after electrical apparatus was introduced.

HIGHLIGHTS

1. Where, when, and by whom was the mask invented?
2. Name three legendary fencing masters responsible for the development of foil fencing in the United States.
3. What two factors led to the popularity of foil fencing?
4. When were the AFLA (USFA) and the USFCA established?
5. As a competitor, what benefits did Michael Marx experience?

BASIC SKILLS

Mastering basic skills is a prerequisite to efficient performance. Skills should be acquired in a logical and progressive sequence. The time it takes to develop each skill depends on the abilities, attitudes, goals, background, and motivation of both the student and the instructor.

When each new skill is learned, it should be combined with previously learned skills. Later you will be able to use the skills in a bout and not be merely a storehouse of isolated skills.

Fencing is a dynamic and mobile sport. Written explanations and discussions of basic skills cannot convey the excitement and vitality of fencing. Therefore, the reader should observe experienced fencers in a competition or on film to note how all the parts of each movement are related and combined in a continuous action. This will give added meaning to the basic skills discussed in this section.

The Basic Foil Positions

The Grip

The ability to hold the foil correctly is the key to good offensive maneuvers. As mentioned before, there are three basic designs for fencing handles: French, Italian, and Belgian (at times called orthopedic or pistol handles). This text refers only to the French-design handle.

The handle of the French foil is shaped and curved to rest comfortably in the hand. Place the first phalanx of the index finger on the underside of the handle close to the bell guard. Then place the thumb flat on the topside of the handle just above the

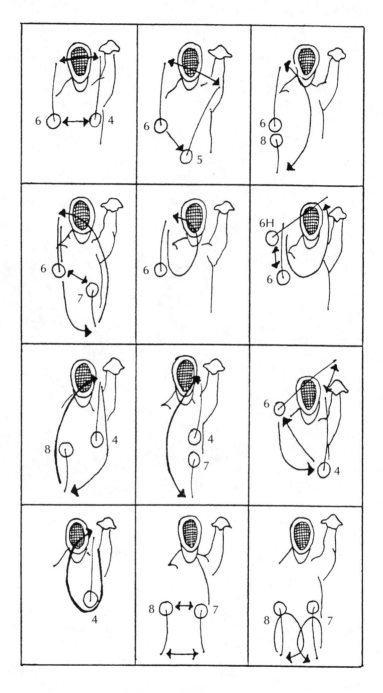

Weapon Position and Change of Position

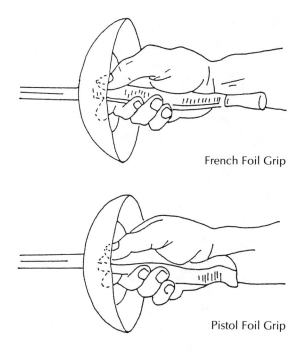

French Foil Grip

Pistol Foil Grip

index finger. The handle now rests against the palm of the hand just beneath the fleshy part of the thumb. Close the remaining three fingers lightly but firmly around the handle.

The thumb and index finger are called the manipulators. They move the point in any direction with a minimum amount of assistance from the wrist, and preferably with none from the arm and shoulder. The three remaining fingers (called aids) are used to control the movement of the blade.

LEARNING EXPERIENCE—GRIP AND FINGERPLAY

1. *Compare a right-handed and a left-handed French foil.*
2. *Grip the foil with only the manipulators. Using only the thumb and index finger, trace the following shapes with the point of the foil:*

3. *Use a doorknob as a point of reference, and draw shapes around it using the three aids to control the movement of the blade.*

The Basic Position (Position of Attention)

The basic position is preparatory to the *salute* and the *on-guard* positions. In the sequence of commands to runners—"On your mark! Get set! Go!"—the "On your mark" position correlates to the basic position (position of attention) in fencing. It is a preparatory position that fencers assume as they salute their opponent with their weapon and don their masks.

Stand erect with feet at right angles. The heel of the rear* foot is placed behind the heel of the leading foot so imaginary right-angle lines drawn will coincide with the inside and outside edges of the rear foot and of the leading foot (see the diagram). The rear arm is extended symmetrically to the weapon arm. The weapon arm is extended with thumbnail at 1 o'clock and the point directed at the opponent's knee. The body is relaxed, with the leading shoulder directed at the opponent.

LEARNING EXPERIENCE—BASIC POSITION

Mark two lines at right angles with chalk or tape. Assume the position of attention. Are your feet placed as shown in the diagram?

Leading Foot, Basic Position

*For the right-handed fencer, "rear" refers to the left foot, leg, shoulder, arm, or hand; "leading" refers to the right.

The Salute

In fencing, the salute is a symbol of goodwill and sportsmanship. A brisk, swashbuck-ling movement of the sword, the salute once signified that a combatant recognized the opponent as worthy and was prepared to defend oneself within the rules of the duel.

Today the salute is brief and brisk, but it remains a symbol of courtesy and sportsmanship, dating back to the days of duelling and chivalry. Many variations of the salute are used at competitions. The salute described below is simple and to the point:

1. Stand at attention on the on-guard line. Hold the mask with the rear hand. Grip the foil. Extend the weapon arm and foil diagonally toward the oppo-nent's knee.
2. Raise the extended arm and foil until they are parallel to the floor, with the tip of the foil directed at the opponent. Flex the elbow, bringing the guard close to the lips, with the tip of the foil pointing upward.
3. With a brisk movement, extend the weapon arm toward the opponent and then back to the initial position.
4. Don the mask and be ready for combat.

The Salute

The On-Guard Position

The on-guard position is the basic stance for all fencers. The expression "On guard" implies that the fencer is ready mentally and physically for action. The position enables the fencer to be mobile and provides the maximum reach while limiting the amount of valid target area presented to the opponent. Because it requires the use of muscles not ordinarily called on to support the body, a fencer may experience initial discomfort until the muscles have been properly conditioned.

On-Guard Position

The on-guard position requires steps that are gradually combined into one continuous movement: Lift arms and step out, flex knees and lower the body to a sitting posture, and position the arms.

1. *"Lift arms."* With both arms in the basic position, simultaneously raise the arms to shoulder level, weapon pointed at opponent. The trailing arm is extended slightly inside the shoulder line. Pretend the bell guard is the face of a clock. The weapon and hand should be toward supination—that is, the thumbnail should be between 12 o'clock and 1:30.

The *"step out"* is executed by moving the leading foot forward so the feet are approximately shoulder-width apart. Keep the weight equally distributed between both feet.

2. The *"sitting posture"* is executed by flexing both knees, with the leading knee over the base of the toes of the leading foot, and the rear knee over and in the same plane with the rear foot. Sit down as if on the edge of a chair or desk, keeping the body erect and the hips in line, as though a plumbline had been dropped from the top of your head to the floor. The center of gravity is now lowered, giving the body greater stability and mobility. Body weight should be equally and centrally distributed.

LEARNING EXPERIENCE—ON-GUARD BODY BALANCE

To attain a perfectly balanced on-guard position, employ the following drill: Extend both arms with palms up to form a straight line from fingertip to fingertip. Assume the on-guard position as described. Alternately and rapidly lift one foot at a time and quickly return to the same position. Your arms should remain level and in line while performing the exercise.

---

3. *"Position your arms."* Both arms are extended. Simultaneously, flex the leading arm, dropping the elbow toward the torso not closer than your hand length (for foil

and épée) or fist length (for saber). Bend the trailing arm at approximately a right angle, with the trailing hand relaxed inwardly. The rear arm is lifted and flexed to form a right angle. Raise the rear arm, flex the elbow; flex the wrist, keeping the fingers relaxed and pointing them toward the opponent. This arm position counterbalances the position of the foil arm.

The fencer should keep the head erect, looking directly at the opponent, to maintain good vision and balance. The point of the weapon should be at the fencer's own eye level or slightly lower.

The weapon arm, positioned between the two opponents, will act as a shield. *The elbow should not be placed outside the bout plane.**

The hipline of the stance is angled at 10–25 degrees to the bout line, providing stability to the fencing position and creating conditions for greater mobility.

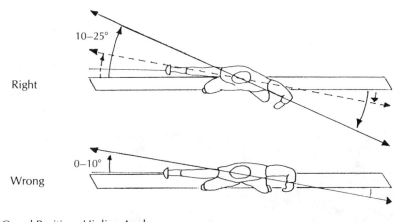

Right

Wrong

On-Guard Position, Hipline Angle

LEARNING EXPERIENCE—ON-GUARD POSITION

1. *Using a full-length mirror, look at your image as you assume the on-guard position. Imagine your image to be an opponent and assume a position that does not expose to your "opponent" any target area on the outside of the blade. This should be your initial on-guard hand position.*

2. *Using a full-length mirror, assume the on-guard position. Is your position similar to that in the illustration?*

---

*The bout line (fencing line) is an imaginary straight line that would pass through the heels of the rear feet and the long axis of the front feet of two adversaries as they face each other in the fencing position. The weapon arms of both fencers are within the same geometrical bout plane (fencing plane) in reference to the bout line. The bout plane (fencing plane) is an imaginary two-dimensional plane that arises from the bout line perpendicular to the fencing strip.

Footwork

Proper footwork is essential for mobility in fencing. By launching attacks quickly and readily moving out of range, a fencer on the move is difficult to hit. In fencing, movement is either forward or backward (advancing or retreating). With a moving target, the attacker must constantly adjust distance, timing, and speed to create the opportunity for a score. The distance covered by an advance or retreat will differ with each situation.

The Advance

An advance, or step forward, is used to close the distance between fencers. Through training, observation, and experience, a fencer will learn to regulate the distance according to an opponent's style and technique.

To execute the advance, lift the toe of the leading foot and step forward approximately one foot length, placing the heel down first. As the ball of the leading foot is set down, the rear foot should be brought forward the same distance covered by the leading foot.

The advance can be executed in a two-count cadence: (1) step forward with the leading foot, landing on the heel, (2) bring up the rear foot and simultaneously set down the ball of the leading foot. For greater mobility, glide rather than drag the feet.

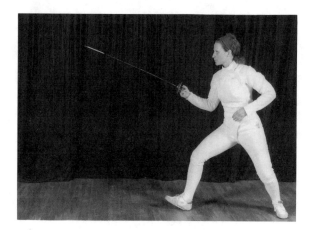

The Advance

The Retreat

A fencer uses the retreat, or step back, to avoid being hit, to maintain distance, or to bait the opponent.

To execute the retreat, extend the rear leg, placing the ball of the rear foot approximately one foot length behind the original position. Bring the leading foot back an equal distance, placing the entire sole of the foot firmly on the floor.

The Retreat

LEARNING EXPERIENCE—ADVANCE AND RETREAT

1. Imagine the ceiling of the fencing room as only a trifle higher than the height of your body in its on-guard position. As you practice the advance and the retreat, avoid lifting your body in a bobbing action that would cause your head to hit the imaginary ceiling. You should move in a horizontal line without wasted effort.
2. Vary the distance of the advances and retreats.
3. Combine the advance and retreat into various patterns, such as advance-retreat, retreat-advance, advance-advance-retreat.
4. How quickly can you execute double advances and/or double retreats—that is, two rapid advances or retreats?
5. Vary the speed of your advance and retreat drills by responding to an established cadence.
6. After executing several advances and retreats, check the distance between your feet to be sure your base of support has been maintained.
7. Close your eyes and listen as you advance and retreat. The sounds you hear should be crisp and decisive.

Extension of Weapon Arm and Lunge

The *extension of the weapon arm* is used to threaten the opponent by moving the point toward the target. In order to score, a foil fencer must hit the opponent with the tip of the foil. To do this, aim at a specific spot on the target and extend your arm. Extension of the weapon arm threatens the opponent, forcing the opponent to defend himself or herself.

With the weapon arm in the on-guard position, extend the arm, raising the hand to shoulder height and keeping the hand slightly toward supination. The pommel of the

Extension of
Weapon Arm

foil lies along the forearm. Because hand movements must be made with split-second timing, it is essential that the extension be a relaxed, smooth, lightning-fast movement. Be careful not to lock the elbow through hyperextension or elevate or hunch the shoulders.

As the arm extension is being completed, flex the wrist slightly, permitting the point of the weapon to descend toward the target. To recover from the extension, flex the elbow and return it to its original position.

LEARNING EXPERIENCE—ARM EXTENSION (THRUST)

1. *Combine the extension with the advance and the retreat: extend, advance, retreat, on-guard.*
2. *Advance with the extension. As the extension begins, advance.*
3. *Repeat the same with the retreat until the movements are smooth, controlled, and rapid.*
4. *Have a fencing partner hold a glove against the wall and release it from varying heights above the fencer's head. Try to pin the glove against a wall mat by extending the foil arm. (The "drop the glove" game can be adapted to many skills for developing reflexes and point control.)*

The *lunge* is a type of footwork designed to enable the fencer to reach the opponent from a distance greater than that offered merely by extension of the weapon arm.

To reach the opponent, extend the foil arm, then propel the body forward by stepping out with the leading foot. Acquire added momentum by vigorously extending the rear leg while keeping the rear foot flat, leaving full print on the floor.

The component movements of the lunge should blend into a smooth, flowing, continuous action, beginning with the leading arm, then the leading leg, the rear leg, and the rear arm.

The Lunge

The leading (weapon) arm initiates the attack. The extension of the weapon arm is one of the most significant skills to master. Movement of the leading foot before extension of the foil arm will give away the attack. Start the attack by extending the foil arm level with the shoulder, stepping forward quickly with the leading leg.

The leading leg then takes an exaggerated walking step forward. When stepping forward, raise the toes slightly and extend the leg, keeping the knee at the same elevation while skimming the heel across the fencing strip. (Land on the heel before setting the ball of the foot down.)

At the completion of the lunge, the lower leg is perpendicular to the floor with the knee over the instep. The trailing leg is completely extended, with the rear foot flat on the floor. The feet are still at right angles, as in the on-guard position.

The length of the lunge may vary with the distance between the fencers.

LEARNING EXPERIENCE—EXTENDING THE LEADING LEG

To acquire the skill of extending your leading leg, place a coin under the leading foot. Lifting the toes and extending the leg while skimming the heel along the strip will propel the coin sharply forward.

The rear leg provides the additional force that propels the body toward the opponent. As the leading leg is extended, the rear leg explosively accelerates the body forward. The rear leg in the lunge can be compared to a compressed coiled spring that imparts energy and force when released.

The rear foot is the source of power and the point from which the lunging distance is measured. It is important that the rear foot remain flat and firm to maintain the desired distance.

The Lunge

1

2

3

To counteract the forward momentum of the body, extend the rear arm smartly to the rear, parallel to the trailing leg, palm up. Any major change from the normal pattern of extending the rear arm will cause the point of the weapon to deviate.

In competition, competitors must strive for favorable distance to perform their determined action. For concluding an offensive or defensive action, proper footwork is essential to establish the correct distance. Action may be executed from short, middle, or long distance.

Short distance allows the fencer to reach the opponent without using footwork.
Middle distance requires the fencer to reach the opponent with simple footwork—the advance, lunge, or flèche.
Long distance requires the fencer to reach the opponent using compound footwork—for example, two advances, advance-lunge, balestra (jump forward–lunge), advance-flèche.

LEARNING EXPERIENCE—THE LUNGE

1. *Use a mirror or a fellow fencer as a critic. From the lunge position (arms resting on the hips), initiate recovery to on-guard by simultaneously flexing the rear knee joint and pulling with the thigh muscle of the trailing leg while pushing back with the heel of the leading leg. Hold on. Initiate the lunge. Hold on. Repeat.*
2. *Repeat #1, but add the following: Extend arms in the lunge position and flex the arms to the on-guard position when imitating recovery.*
3. *Repeat the preceding: recover, lunge, recover, lunge.*
4. *Practice ten lunges, holding the position after each lunge. Check and correct the position of each body part. Remember to keep your trunk erect and your body weight equally distributed on both legs.*

How do you feel? Uncomfortable? Muscles straining? If the lunge is executed as described, you may be uncomfortable. In the initial learning stages, the physical demands of the lunge are severe, but the muscles can adapt to the demands if appropriate conditioning measures are used.

Recovery to the on-guard position is made either to the rear (the rear leg remaining stationary) or forward (with the leading leg stationary). The fencer should not remain in the lunge position, so he or she must be prepared to recover quickly.

To recover to the rear from a lunge, flex the rear knee first. Pull back with the rear knee joint and support it by pushing off with the heel of the leading foot to return to the original on-guard position. Return the rear arm and the weapon arm to their original positions.

To recover forward from a lunge, flex the rear knee, bring the rear leg forward to a wider on-guard position, and at the same time flex the rear arm. The leading arm may remain extended or return to the on-guard position, depending on the opponent's

The Lunge: Recovery
to the Guard Position

1

2

3

reaction. The center of gravity at this moment is slightly lower, permitting the fencer to renew the attack with greater velocity.

LEARNING EXPERIENCE—LUNGE, RECOVERY, AND FOOTWORK

1. *Practice five lunges with immediate recovery to the rear.*
2. *Practice five lunges with immediate recovery forward.*
3. *Combine all the footwork learned thus far into sequential drills, such as advance-retreat-extend-lunge-recover forward; double retreat-advance-extend-lunge-recover to the rear.*
4. *Vary the tempo at which the combinations are executed, by increasing the speed gradually while still retaining efficient form.*
5. *Holding the foil, practice various drills employing the retreat, advance, lunge, and recovery. Ask the following questions while practicing:*
    a. *Is the tip motionless?*
    b. *Do the weapon, the hand, and the forearm form a straight line from the tip of the elbow to the tip of the blade?*
    c. *Is the tip of the foil at eye level?*
    d. *Is the wrist firm and straight?*
    e. *Is the thumb in the correct position?*
    f. *Is the elbow of the leading arm in the proper position?*

Target Areas and Fencing Lines

Four sectors, or target areas—outside high, outside low, inside high, and inside low—are formed by two imaginary lines, horizontal and vertical, intersecting at the bell guard.

The four lines or areas are used to discover the relationship between the hand with the weapon and the target and to understand defensive positions with regard to the target.

When the weapon is held in a central guard position and the thumbnail is directed at 12 o'clock, the high line is the area above the bell guard, and the low line is below the bell guard.

The *outside high line* is an imaginary line that would connect the farthest point of the extended weapon hand above the guard to the most extreme point of the fencer's backside target area as one stands in the fencing position.

The *inside high line* is an imaginary line that would connect the farthest point of the extended weapon hand above the guard to the most extreme point on the fencer's chest target area as one stands in the fencing position.

Accordingly, the *outside and inside low lines* are conceived the same way as the high lines, but below the guard, thus establishing four areas of reference: the outside high line, the outside low line, the inside high line, and the inside low line.

It is impossible to protect the entire target area at one time. For example, when protecting (or closing) the outside high line, the other three areas are unprotected (or open). Likewise, if the inside high line is protected or closed, the inside low, outside high, and outside low lines are unprotected or open and therefore subject to attack.

Target Area Protection

Target Area	Protected By
Outside High Line	3rd and 6th positions
Inside High Line	4th and 5th positions
Outside Low Line	8th and 2nd positions
Inside Low Line	7th and 1st positions

In order to protect a specific area, the hand and foil are placed in certain positions, numbered 1 through 8 for purposes of identification.

The Protection Positions

"Position" is the placement of the weapon in any of four lines related to the covered target area. The position number describes the spatial relationship between the fencer's weapon and the general target area it covers.

The term "parry" describes the relationship between two opponents' weapons when one directs his or her blade to a specific target area against the other's blade. The placement of a parry changes along the lines because the depth and the angle of an opponent's attack varies. Position and parry coincide when an opponent attacks into a line that has already been secured by a position (a closed line).

The hand may be supinated (palm up) or pronated (palm down); correspondingly, the blade may be above the hand or below. The table of protection positions shows which of the eight positions protects each area.

Protection Positions

Position	Hand	Point of Blade	Area Protected
First	Overpronated	Below guard	Inside low
Second	Overpronated	Below guard	Outside low
Third	Pronated	Above guard	Outside high
Fourth	Toward pronation	Above guard	Inside high
Fifth	Pronated	Above guard	Inside high
Sixth	Toward supination	Above guard	Outside high
Seventh	Supinated	Below guard	Inside low
Eighth	Supinated	Below Guard	Outside low

Beginner's Positions

Of the eight positions, four are common: 4th, 6th, 7th, and 8th. The other four are used less frequently.

Position 6

By becoming familiar with just two positions—4th and 6th—a beginning fencer will be able to develop a basic defense. These are also the positions the most-skilled fencers use most frequently.

6th Position. The weapon hand should have the thumb between 12 and 2 o'clock and the blade covering (protecting) the outside high line for a right-handed fencer.

Position 4

4th Position. The weapon hand should have the thumb between 12 and 11 o'clock and the blade covering (protecting) the inside high line for a right-handed fencer.

Some instructors teach slight variations in the hand and blade positions, advocating various degrees of pronation of the hand (turning the palm down) as the fencer moves from 6th to 4th position. The authors suggest that the hand turn toward supination when moving from 4th to 6th position, and toward pronation when moving from 6th to 4th, for more strength and better point and blade control.

LEARNING EXPERIENCE—6TH AND 4TH POSITIONS

Stand in front of a mirror. The image you see will be similar to that of an opponent facing you.

1. *On-guard.*
2. *Move the weapon arm to 6th position to protect the outside high line. Look into the mirror at your "opponent." If any part of the target area is visible in the outside high line, the position is not correct and the target area is not protected from an attack into this line. Be sure the entire target area in 6th position is covered.*
3. *Repeat with the 4th position.*

Note: Avoid exaggerated lateral movements that resemble a windshield wiper when changing from 6th to 4th and back.

Speed and simplicity are paramount in fencing today. Avoid becoming enamored of highly involved movements except as an exercise for developing quick responses and facile fingerplay. After acquiring skills and knowledge, fence often and against many right-handed and left-handed opponents. It is through bouting that fencers can develop their skills and test their analytical ability, timing, sense of distance, and speed.

The Simple Attacks

Attacks (either simple or compound) are aggressive actions intended to score against the opponent while progressively delivering the point of the weapon to the target.

Simple attacks are attacks that are executed in one "fencing time"—that is, on the way to the target the point executes no more than a single movement. The simple attacks may be *direct* or *indirect*.

Simple Direct Attack

A *simple direct attack* is an action into the line of engagement or, if there is no engagement, without change of a line. A *simple indirect attack* is an action into the opposite line of engagement. Both involve a single blade movement, the straight thrust.

The *straight thrust* (arm extension) is a simple direct attack and may be used with or without footwork. Its execution has already been covered in this chapter, but it is important to emphasize that speed, proper timing, and accuracy are essential for success. Constant practice is necessary to coordinate the extension of the weapon arm with the lunge. This attack must be executed with precision without revealing one's intention.

Attack with Lunge

LEARNING EXPERIENCE—SIMPLE DIRECT ATTACKS

1. *Engage the blades in 6th position.*
   Fencer A: Move blade to 4th position.
   Fencer B: Execute a straight thrust and lunge.

2. *Engage the blades in 4th position.*
   Fencer A: *Extend weapon arm as though intending to attack, but return instead to the original position.*
   Fencer B: *Execute a straight thrust and lunge as Fencer A begins the return to the original position.*
3. *In the absence of blade contact—*
   Fencer A: *Put weapon in 8th position.*
   Fencer B: *Execute a straight thrust and lunge into the higher target area.*

Simple Indirect Attacks

The simple attack that starts from the position of engagement and lands to the open areas of the target with the help of the disengage or cutover is called the *indirect attack*.

The *disengage* is a passing movement of the blade to avoid engagement or any contact with the opponent's blade by passing under or over the strong part of the opponent's blade (forté). When in the high line, the disengage is executed under the opponent's blade. When in the low line, it is accomplished by passing over the opponent's blade.

The *disengagement* is a simple indirect attack employing the disengage, where a blade moves from the line of engagement into the opposite open line in one continuous, fluid motion. It is the most frequently used attack and must be mastered for success in fencing.

Executing the Disengagement

The disengagement requires finger control. Lowering the point on one side and lifting the point on the other side are accomplished by alternately relaxing and tightening the grip without any lateral movement of the arm. The most effective point movement is in the shape of a Y, keeping the point constantly on target, rather than a broad or circular U, which may cause the point to move off the target.

Executing the disengagement is comparable to inserting a light bulb in a socket. The bulb is moving both forward and in a circle. In a disengagement, the point is continually moving forward even as it descends on the one side and ascends on the other. The hand remains in the original position.

LEARNING EXPERIENCE*—DISENGAGEMENT

1. *Engage the blades in 6th position. Disengage to the inside high line with a bent arm, concentrating on finger movement.*
2. *Engage the blades in 6th position. Disengage to the inside high line, extending*

---

*The Learning Experience in this concept and in all others in this book are for two right-handed fencers.

the arm as the point is lowered and then rises. The guard should move directly toward the target.

3. On-guard in 6th position. Maintain absence of blade contact. As the opponent moves the weapon laterally from 4th to 6th position, deceive it—disengage before contact is made with your blade. (Performing the disengage successfully is the beginning of learning the art of deception, which is so vital to the enjoyment and success of fencing.)

4. Repeat the same sequence with the 4th position. (The area of the disengagement is determined by the path the point must take around the opponent's blade and by the distance to the target.)

5. Fencer A: Slowly change engagement from 6th to 4th position and back to 6th.
    Fencer B: As the change begins, start disengagement (deceiving the opponent's attempt to engage blades), extend, and lunge.

Executing the Cutover

The *cutover attack* is an inverted disengagement. Instead of passing beneath the opponent's forté, the cutover passes over the tip of the opponent's weapon, ending in the line opposite the engagement.

As the weapon is drawn back slightly to pass over the opponent's point, the forearm is raised partially with a slight flexing of the wrist. As soon as the tip of the opponent's blade is cleared, smartly extend the forearm down and forward, threatening the target on the other side of the blade. The entire action must be swift and decisive. Indecision or faulty execution may give the opponent an opportunity to counterattack.

LEARNING EXPERIENCE—THE CUTOVER

1. Engage the blades in 4th position.
    Fencer A: Press the opponent's blade.
    Fencer B: Cutover while extending, and lunge.
2. Engage the blades in 6th position.
    Fencer A: Start to change engagement.
    Fencer B: Cutover while extending, and lunge.

The Engagement and Change of Engagement

The contact of the blades is called *engagement*. The purpose of engaging an opponent's blade is to determine whether the weapon is being held loosely or tightly. (*Note:* The opposite of engagement of blades is termed *absence of blades*, or absence of blade contact.)

Blades are engaged according to fencing lines. For example, an engagement in 6th position means the blades are crossed in outside high line—that is, the fencers, if

Engagement in 6
with Advance

they are both right-handed or both left-handed, have their high outside line protected. Each fencer in this case has the other lines open. Therefore, if both fencers are
engaged in 6th and either one extends and/or lunges into high outside, the valid
target should be covered.

The *change of engagement* (engaging in a new line) adds variety to a fencer's
repertoire.

Change of engagement (from 4th to 6th position or from 6th to 4th) is executed by
passing the point under the opposing blade (in a manner similar to that of the
disengage) and moving the hand into the line of opposition. Such a movement brings
the point into the opponent's open line while still holding the opponent's blade.

This skill enables a fencer to move quickly from one line to another, keeping the
opponent in doubt as to what the next move will be. The development of a more
extensive repertoire of movements makes the fencer less predictable and more difficult to defeat.

LEARNING EXPERIENCE—CHANGE OF ENGAGEMENT

1. *Engage the blades in 6th position.*
    a. *Change the engagement into 4th position.*
    b. *Change the engagement while advancing (1) as the leading foot is moving
        and (2) as rear foot completes the advance.*
    c. *Retreat with the change of engagement.*
    d. *Advance with the change of engagement, extend, and lunge.*
2. *Engage the blades in 4th position and repeat.*

The *double change of engagement* adds still more variety to the fencer's repertoire.
The double change of engagement consists of changing engagement from one line to
another and then back to the original line. The first change is a crisp action. The
second is a holding or sustained action similar to the single change.

---

1. *Repeat #1 of the Learning Experience for change of engagement, with a double change instead of a single.*
2. *Engage the blades in 6th position. Add mobility to the double change. Advance and double change. The leading foot moves with the first change of engagement (beat), the rear foot moves with the second change of engagement (hold).*

Parries and Ripostes

Parries block attacks by deflecting the opponent's blade. They are different geometrically (lateral, semicircular, or circular) and by the character of their impact (block, beat, pressure, or yield). At this time we introduce the most common types of parries.

The Blocking Parry

The blocking parry 4 is used to defend against an attack coming into the inside high line. The hand is moving toward pronation and stops the rotation of the wrist when the thumbnail arrives between 12 and 11 o'clock and the point is directed approximately toward the right ear of opponent—the blade thus blocking that defensive line.

It would be folly to reach for the opponent's blade if it were not threatening the target. A fencer should parry as though building a sturdy wall for protection against an onslaught. The parry needs the force of forearm, wrist, and blade.

The blocking parry 6 is used to defend against an attack into the outside high line. The action requires coordinated movement of the hand and forearm toward supination pivoting from the elbow. The blade closes the outside high line by contacting the opponent's blade with a sustained action. All learning experiences for parry 4 can be used for learning parry 6.

The Beat Parry

The beat parry is different from the blocking parry because of its tactical application and therefore also its technical execution. The beat parry generally *prevents* final movement of the attack; the blocking parry is used mostly against the final movement of the attack.

The Lateral Parry

A fencer can defend with a lateral parry by moving the blade laterally across the body. Only after successfully parrying the attack may a fencer initiate an attack. The theory behind this is simple. If fencers used lethal weapons, it would be suicidal to attack while being attacked.

The lateral high-line parries 4 and 6 can be executed (1) either by moving the hand as well as the blade to *block* the opponent's threat (a *blocking parry*) or (2) by executing a crisp, persuasive *beat* to bounce the opponent's blade away (a *beat parry*).

Parry 6

The Circular or Counter-Parry

The circular parry, or counter-parry, is a near ellipse (down and around), picking up the opponent's blade and carrying it back to the original line of engagement. The circular parry 6 is executed in a clockwise direction for right-handed fencers. The circular parry 4 is executed in a counterclockwise fashion for right-handed fencers. The effect is a "digging" movement (down and under). The circular movement is

Position 6 High

made in relation to the opponent's blade—that is, if the attack is high the defender will not have to dig as much as if the blade were lower. Because of the distance the point travels in executing the parry, it requires a longer time to execute, but it will protect a larger area.

The Parry-Riposte

A riposte is an attack executed immediately after a successful parry. Riposte gives a fencer the right of way, and the key word is *immediately*. A parry that is held without a riposte may enable the opponent to persist in attacking.

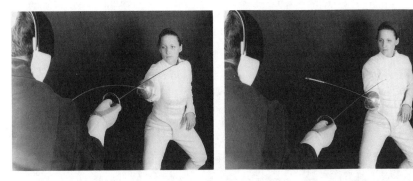

Riposte with Opposition 4   Parry 4

LEARNING EXPERIENCE—PARRIES AND RIPOSTES

Reciprocal exercises in which each person has a specific role provide the basis for learning fencing techniques. Fencers should use the early exercise periods as training sessions, not as simulated bouting experience. Each fencing movement has a certain rhythm. Only when a novice feels the rhythm of a movement should an attempt be made to execute it more rapidly.

1. *On-guard in 6th position, no engagement, middle distance.*
   Fencer A: Attack straight with extension.
   Fencer B: Parry 4, no riposte.
2. *Same position.*
   Fencer A: Attack straight with advance.
   Fencer B: Parry 4 and riposte with extension of blade arm.
3. *Same position.*
   Fencer A: Attack straight with lunge and remain in lunge position.
   Fencer B: Do small retreat with parry 4 and riposte directly with extension.

4.   *Same position.*
     Fencer A: Attack straight with lunge and recover immediately.
     Fencer B: Retreat parrying 4 and riposte directly with lunge.
5.   *Practice the above also from the positions of engagement in 4th or 6th position.*
6.   *Practice the same progression to help your partner respond by using circular parries.*

The Feint, a Compound Attack

A *feint-attack* is a mock attack toward one area with the intention of striking another portion of the target. In boxing, a feint to the belly may culminate in a blow to the head. In fencing a feint may be executed with any portion of the body, as in other sports, but feints are usually made with the weapon, to draw a defensive reaction.

An extension of the blade toward a valid target can be a feint. If the opponent responds to the feint with a lateral or circular motion, a fencer can deceive the attempt to parry.

Manipulate the weapon using only the fingers in order to deceive the opponent. The bell guard, arm, and hand should not change position. They should continue to move forward, giving the impression of a straight attack.

Straight Feint

LEARNING EXPERIENCE—FEINTS

1.   *Practice a full extension (a feint) with vigor to help create a threatening situation. The opponent responds to the attacker's feint; the attacker deceives the opponent's blade.*
2.   *On-guard in 6th position (also practice in 4th).*

Fencer A: Extend into the inside high line (or outside high line).
Fencer B: Parry lateral 4 (or parry lateral 6).
Fencer A: Deceive with a disengage and lunge.
3. On-guard in 6th position (also practice in 4th).
    Fencer A: Extend into the inside high line (or outside high line).
    Fencer B: Attempt a circular 6 parry (or circular 4 parry).
    Fencer A: Deceive (following the direction of the opponent's blade) and lunge.
4. To learn to execute a feint, first make a simple attack with a lunge against a
    stationary opponent. Practice the same attack, but with an advance. This is a
    proper feint. Watch yourself in a mirror to see whether your feint resembles a
    real attack.

Attacks with the Action on the Blade

The beat, change beat, transfer, take-the-blade, and pressure are actions against an
opponent's blade that prepare the way for an attack.

The Beat Attack

The beat attack is a sharp, crisp action made against the weaker part of the opponent's blade for the purpose of gaining "right-of-way." This attack is particularly
successful against a fencer who consistently has the foil arm extended.

To execute the beat, relax the pressure on the grip and then contract your fingers
with a very slight wrist and forearm action. The contact with the opponent's blade
should be decisive but not excessive. At the moment of contact, the point of the
blade is still approximately eye-high, so that an extension of the weapon will bring
the point to the target.

LEARNING EXPERIENCE—THE BEAT ATTACK

*The progression used in learning the beat attack can be applied to learning all
attacks:*

1. *On-guard in 6th position.*
2. *Beat in 4th position against another blade to get the feeling.*
3. *Beat in 4th against another blade and extend.*
4. *Beat in 4th and extend against an extended blade.*
5. *Beat in 4th, extend, and lunge.*
6. *Advance and beat in 4th, extend-lunge.*
7. *Retreat and beat in 4th, extend-lunge.*

The same progression can be used to practice beats in 6th, 7th, and 8th position.

The Change-Beat Attack

The change-beat attack is executed the same way as the first change in the double change of engagement—that is, by relaxing the grip, moving the point to a new line, and firmly gripping the handle to beat the blade crisply. The fencer can follow this action with a straight thrust.

---

1. *Engage the blades in 6th position (also practice in 4th).*
   a.   *Change beat 4.*
   b.   *Change beat 4, extend.*
   c.   *Change beat 4, extend and lunge.*
2. *Engage in 4th position (also practice in 6th). Add mobility by advancing with the change beat and extension. The synchronized actions should be as follows: no blade action with the leading foot, beat is executed as the rear foot lands, extend-lunge.*

The Transfer

The transfer (or bind) is executed by taking the opponent's blade from high line into opposite diagonal low line without releasing contact at any time. It can be executed in similar fashion from low line to opposite diagonal high line. Several examples include transferring (binding) from 6th to 7th position, from 4th to 2nd or 8th position, and from 7th to 6th position.

The Take-the-Blade Attack (Glide)

Taking the blade is an action of seizing the opponent's blade and controlling it to its conclusion. There are four such attacks, and all have two prerequisites:

1.   The opponent's blade should be in an almost horizontal position.
2.   The opponent's weapon arm should be fully extended or almost fully extended.

The four attacks are:

1.   The *glide,* which can be executed with or without *opposition.*
2.   The *envelopment,* which is the taking of the blade in one line and controlling it while remaining in the same line, at the same time executing a wide circular motion of the blade. Blade remains in contact while the point moves toward the target.
3.   The *bind,* an action of taking the opponent's blade from a high line and bringing it into the opposite diagonal low line without releasing it at any time. The bind can also be executed from low to high line.

4. The *croisé* (cross), a semibind executed by taking the opponent's blade vertically from the high line to the low line. Example: taking the blade from 4th to 7th position, or from 6th to 8th position.

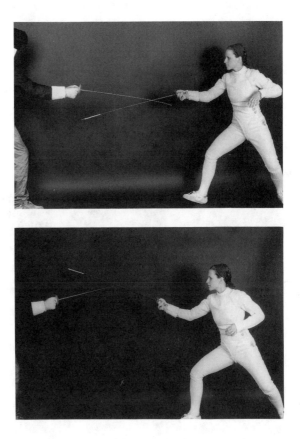

Take-the-Blade in 7
with Advance

Take-the-Blade in 4
with Advance

Pressure

The opponent's blade can be deflected by pressing it aside. Imagine a cat crouching until the moment it springs. This movement is attack with opposition in which a fencer presses the foible of the opponent's blade, maintains the pressure until he or she senses the tactile reaction, and then springs to the target.

To add decisiveness to the attack, start the leading foot just slightly before releasing the opponent's blade. If the opponent reacts by pressing in return, follow the preparatory action with a disengage.

The purpose of these preparatory movements is to elicit a reaction from the opponent. A fencer must be prepared to deal with that reaction:

If the opponent resists the pressure or the glide or reacts to the beat, deceive the movement with a disengage.

If the opponent yields to the take-the-blade, execute a circular movement to deceive the blade.

If the opponent does not respond at all, go straight to the target.

A victim of a preparatory movement must be prepared to defend against it:

Do not maintain an extended-arm position unless inviting the opponent to act against the blade.

Evade the blade as the opponent initiates the action.

A counterpreparatory movement can be successful against an opponent whose preparatory movements are indecisive—for example, your adversary presses against the blade. A quick counterpressure-attack may take the opponent by surprise.

Distance and Timing

The *fencing distance* is the physical relationship between two adversaries. Because fencers differ in height, flexibility, and arm and leg length, sense of distance becomes an important skill in competition. The ability to gain or break (change) the distance requires excellent footwork and a precise evaluation of one's own distance to attack. A fencer uses footwork to get within reach or out of reach of the opponent.

"Distance" is the interval separating two fencers. It is maintained by advancing (gaining ground) or retreating (yielding ground).

Timing complements fencing distance and is the ability to seize an opportunity to act against the opponent at the right moment. Choosing the right moment to act is important because every offensive action can be defended if the defender has sufficient reaction time or a sense of timing. Speed is important and necessary, but unless you can adjust your timing to that of your opponent, speed can be wasted and result in an uncontrolled, poorly timed, and ineffective action.

HIGHLIGHTS

1. Demonstrate the proper way to grip a French foil and to manipulate the point.
2. Holding the mask and foil, assume a position of attention and execute a salute. Explain the purpose of the salute.
3. Describe the two steps of the on-guard position. Explain why a fencer assumes this basic position.
4. Describe the two steps in executing the advance and demonstrate a series of three advances. Do the same for the retreat.
5. Demonstrate how to extend the weapon arm and recover.
6. Demonstrate a lunge with recovery forward and recovery to the rear.
7. State the number of positions in which the hand and foil may be placed to protect the target. Demonstrate which are the most basic positions for the beginner.
8. Demonstrate a disengagement from 6th to 4th position and explain how it is accomplished with the fingers.
9. With another fencer, execute a double change of engagement from 6th to 4th and back.
10. With another fencer attacking with the lunge into inside high line, then in the outside high line, execute the appropriate circular and lateral parries.
11. Define riposte and state its function.
12. State the purpose of the feint and the main feature to consider in its execution.
13. Against an opponent's blade, execute each of the beats and the take-the-blade.
14. List three ways to counter these preparatory movements.
15. Differentiate between the simple direct attack and the simple indirect attack.
16. Differentiate between the disengage and the cutover.
17. Define fencing distance, and state two ways of maintaining it.
18. Explain the importance of timing.

ADVANCED SKILLS

Additional attacks, parries, ripostes, preparatory actions, counterattacks, and footwork add interest, variety, excitement, and competitive skill to a fencer's game. Many years ago, fencing masters would insist that beginners spend at least a year on fundamental movements. Only after an adequate period of practice and instruction would a novice be allowed to compete in a tournament. This policy was intended to allow sufficient time for molding the "correct" habits to "ensure" top performance.

Because no two individuals respond alike, the perception of which habits are "correct" and which are not is subjective and tends to be determined either by the pleasing aesthetic qualities of a fencer's movements or by the fencer's success—or both. The aesthetic quality or "proper" form may take years of practice for some to achieve, and only a short time for others.

Only when the fundamentals have been mastered should a fencer move on to new skills. And no matter how skilled or successful a fencer becomes, it is necessary to review and hone the fundamental movements frequently. Programs of advanced skills aim to improve actions already learned, to increase the repertoire of actions, and to develop confidence and the ability for self-analysis.

Adding New Skills and Techniques

New skills and techniques, whether on a beginning or advanced level, should be related to the total game as quickly as possible by adopting three general principles:

1. Observe the component parts of the skill and how they are similar to the skills already learned.
2. Know how, when, and why the skill is used.
   a. Observe yourself in a mirror while performing the skills.
   b. Add footwork (advance, retreat, lunge) to each new hand skill so that foot and hand movements are coordinated.
   c. Increase the tempo of the movements.
   d. Know all possible responses the opponent might make, and practice counterresponses.

e.   Practice the newly acquired skill during bouts in class.
3.   While executing the skills, aspire to technical perfection and tactical correctness.

A skill used many times becomes part of the fencer.

Advanced Footwork

Advanced footwork enables a fencer to execute the balestra and the flèche attacks.

The Balestra

The balestra (jump-and-lunge) is similar to the advance but is performed more explosively and quickly. The fencer begins by forcefully swinging (extending) the leading
foreleg without elevating the leading knee. As the leading leg is stretched, the rear
foot is quickly moved forward a distance equal to that covered by the leading foot.
Both feet should land simultaneously. The lunge starts immediately after jump is
completed.

First Phase of Balestra,
Jump Forward

LEARNING EXPERIENCE—THE BALESTRA

1.   *Observe yourself in a mirror. As you perform the balestra, do you move toward
your opponent in a plane parallel to the floor, or do you jump in a parabolic
manner? How much of the sole of your leading foot can you see in the mirror?
The higher you elevate your foot, the slower the execution of the balestra, giving
your opponent the opportunity to recognize your attacking intention and react
accordingly.*
2.   *Extend your weapon arm as you practice a jump forward followed immediately
by a lunge. Check your performance in the mirror.*

The Flèche

The flèche is a fast attack from middle or long distance in which the fencer leaps forward by a leaning-running action that, as a rule, causes one to pass the opponent.

It is important to note that after completing the flèche the fencer becomes vulnerable because it is almost impossible to start a new action. Upon reversing one's fencing position, the opponent has an opportunity to score by executing an immediate riposte. The flèche has an advantage over the balestra or advance-lunge attacks because it can be executed in one fencing time. It becomes very difficult to score with a counterattack against it.

Flèche

The execution of a flèche resembles a prolonged cross-advance. As it starts, the weight is smoothly shifted forward, ahead of the leading foot, until the balance is lost. The rear leg initiates the flèche, but the ball of the leading foot provides the explosive impulse needed to drive the fencer toward the opponent and leave the floor. The extension of the leading leg immediately follows the driving action. As in running, the rear leg then crosses over the leading leg, helping the fencer regain balance and pass rather than collide with the opponent. A fencer should avoid body contact with the opponent.

The hit should score when the leading foot is extending, and not later than the landing of the rear foot. In a flèche, the back toes should be pointed forward, the shoulders remaining parallel to the floor. If the shoulder line changes, the back hip will tend to rise, causing the flèche to be shorter, higher, and as a result slower.

LEARNING EXPERIENCE—THE FLÈCHE

Practice in slow motion the following sequence of movements starting from the on-guard position:

1. *Shift weight to the leading foot, thrust and score.*
2. *To regain balance, cross-advance.*
3. *On-guard.*
4. *Repeat # 1, 2, and 3 with gradually increasing distance and speed.*

Advanced Attacks and Parries

The Low-Line Attack

Low-line attacks are directed at the target area below the bell guard. With the advent of electrical fencing, low-line attacks and parries have become popular, necessary, and effective. Even though a foil point directed under the arm may not be visible to the fencer, the hit will be detected by the electrical scoring machine, which signals the referee that a hit has been made. For that reason, many instructors believe that the low-line attacks and parries should be taught early in the fencing progression.

Attacks to the low line are generally made—

When the opponent's foil hand is high.

When a change in strategy is indicated.

When a fencer wants to open the high line by drawing the opponent into the low line.

Low-Line Attack

To execute low-line attacks, direct the point below the opponent's guard toward the elbow. The arm is lowered with the final movement. The blade should bend laterally on contact with the target to avoid the opponent's arm. The blade will bend laterally if the fencer finishes with the hand in supination (for an attack to the groin area, inside low line) or pronation (for an attack to the flank, outside low line).

LEARNING EXPERIENCE—LOW-LINE ATTACKS

Execute the following with footwork:

1. *Fencer A: Attempt to engage blades in 6th position.*
   Fencer B: Disengage into the groin area, lunge, and score.
2. *Fencer A: Attempt to engage blades in 4th position.*
   Fencer B: Disengage into the flank area, lunge, and score.

Semicircular Parries

In a semicircular parry, parry 7 or parry 8, the point of the weapon describes a sweeping arc as the blade moves from the high line to the low line or vice versa.

Parry 8. When engaged in 6th position and threatened by a low-line attack, the fencer should parry by describing a near semicircle or arc with the point moving counterclockwise for a right-handed fencer. The hand is supinated throughout the parry. Riposte either to the low line or the high line.

Position 8   Position 7

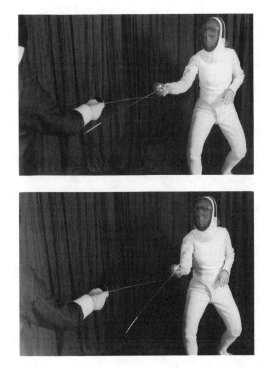

Parry from 6 to 8

Parry from 4 to 7

Parry 7. When engaged in 4th position and threatened in the low line, the fencer should parry by describing a near semicircle or arc with the point moving clockwise for a right-handed fencer. In parry 7, the arc is rounded because it sweeps the point off target. The hand is supinated throughout the parry. Riposte either to the low line or the high line.

The various combinations of semicircular parries are from 6 to 8, from 8 to 6, from 4 to 7, and from 7 to 4. Combinations of parries from 6 to 7 and from 4 to 8 are also very promising but require more experience.

LEARNING EXPERIENCE—LOW-LINE AND SEMICIRCULAR PARRIES

1. *Engage the blades in 6th position.*
   Fencer A: Disengage into the outside low line.
   Fencer B: Execute semicircular parry 8 (and riposte).
2. *Engage in 8th position.*
   Fencer A: Disengage into high line.
   Fencer B: Execute semicircular parry 6 (and riposte).
3. *Repeat the exercise with engagement in 4th and 7th.*

Compound Attacks

The compound attack consists of one or more feints and may be used when a simple attack fails to score because of the strong defensive reaction of the opponent.

A fencer must gain distance on one's opponent at the beginning of the attack by initiating the feint. To resemble the real attack, the feint must penetrate as deeply as possible, threatening the target before the fencer starts the final action.

Having mastered the direct thrust, the disengage, and the cutover, a fencer has acquired the foundation for compound attacks. Developing and successfully executing compound attacks will require practice to coordinate the blade movements, the weapon-arm extension, and the footwork. As a fencer becomes more adept in using compound attacks, the partner should concentrate on increasing the speed of the parry, making an honest effort to contact the fencer's blade.

The One-Two Attack

The one-two attack consists of two disengages. The first disengage is a feint into the open line. The second disengage deceives the opponent's lateral parry—that is, as the opponent parries the disengage, the fencer evades the parry by returning to or disengaging into the original line of engagement.

"The shortest distance between two points is a straight line" is an axiom that can be applied to the one-two attack. The blade and arm move straight forward. Use only the fingers as manipulators to lower and raise the point. When the one-two has been learned, it can be combined with other basic skills.

LEARNING EXPERIENCE—THE ONE-TWO ATTACK

1. *Engage the blades in 6th position.*
    Fencer A: Feint with disengage into inside high line.
    Fencer B: Parry 4.
    Fencer A: Disengage into the outside high line, evading the parry, and score.
2. *Engage in 4th position.*
    Fencer A: Feint with disengage into the outside high line.
    Fencer B: Parry 6.
    Fencer A: Disengage into the inside high line, evading the parry, and score.

Low-High and High-Low Attacks

Low-high and high-low attacks are designed to deceive the semicircular parries.

The low-high attack is begun from an engagement in the high line. The feint to the low line is directed beneath and parallel to the opponent's arm. As the opponent executes the semicircular parry, the fencer should deceive the blade by disengaging into the high line.

The high-low attack starts from an engagement in the low line. The feint is made to the high line. The fencer should deceive the opponent's parry, scoring in the low line.

Doublés

The doublé is a two-part attack used to deceive a circular parry. In the doublé, the first action is a feint with disengage intended to draw the opponent's circular parry. The second action is a circular motion to deceive the circular parry. The blade should remain ahead of the opponent's circular movement while progressing toward the target. The fencer's point describes a continuous circle and a half, ending in the same line into which the feint was made.

LEARNING EXPERIENCE—DOUBLÉ ATTACK

1. *Engage the blades in 6th position.*
   Fencer A: Feint with disengage into the inside high line.
   Fencer B: Circular parry 6.
   Fencer A: Deceive the parry, and score.
2. *Engage in 4th position.*
   Fencer A: Feint with disengage into outside high line.
   Fencer B: Parry circular 4.
   Fencer A: Deceive the parry, and score.

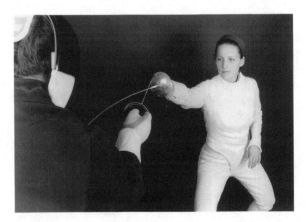

Straight Thrust Riposte
with Opposition 6

Compound Ripostes

A compound riposte consists of one or more feints while making the riposte. To execute the compound riposte successfully, a fencer should delay the lunge, allowing sufficient time for completing the feint(s).

The compound riposte has many variations built around the *extension,* the *disengage,* and the *cutover.*

The primary difference between compound attacks and compound ripostes is that in compound attacks the weapon arm is more fully extended in the feints, while in compound ripostes the weapon arm is extended only on the final movement. (A compound fencing action, whether an attack or a riposte, is merely a combination of simple actions.)

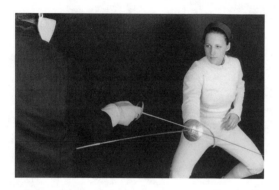

Riposte with Opposition 5

LEARNING EXPERIENCE—COMPOUND RIPOSTE

1. Engage the blades in 6th position, middle distance.
   Fencer A: Attack with a disengage.
   Fencer B: Parry with circular 6.
   Fencer A: Anticipating direct riposte, parry 6.
   Fencer B: Deceive parry 6, feint with disengage (one).
   Fencer A: Parry 4.
   Fencer B: Deceive parry 4 with a disengage (two), and score.
2. Engage in 6th position, middle distance.
   Fencer A: Attack with a disengage.
   Fencer B: Parry with circular 6.
   Fencer A: Anticipating direct riposte, parry 6.
   Fencer B: Deceive parry 6, feint with a disengage.
   Fencer A: Parry circular 6.
   Fencer B: Deceive circular 6 by doubling through with final movement, and score.

Secondary or Renewed Attacks

The remise, reprise, and the redoublement are renewed attacks executed against an opponent whose parry and/or riposte is not decisive. A fencer who doggedly pursues and renews an attack will score many more touches than the fencer who attacks and, missing or falling short, breaks off the attack and recovers before initiating another attack.

The Remise

The remise is a replacement of the point on the target while the attacker is still in the lunge. It is used against an opponent who parries but hesitates, who fails to riposte, or who uses compound ripostes. Immediately following the opponent's parry, the point is directed in the same line as the original attack.

LEARNING EXPERIENCE—THE REMISE

Engage the blades in 6th position.
Fencer A: Disengage and lunge.
Fencer B: Parry 4 and return to central guard position without riposting.
Fencer A: Replace the point on target in the inside line.

The Reprise

The reprise is a new indirect attack (either with disengage or cutover) against an opponent who delays or fails to riposte. It is executed while a fencer is still in the lunge.

LEARNING EXPERIENCE—THE REPRISE

Engage the blades in 6th position.
Fencer A: Disengage and lunge.
Fencer B: Parry 4 and hold the parry.
Fencer A: While in lunge, disengage and score.

The Redoublement

The redoublement is a renewed attack against a fencer who uses passive defense by retreating or who does not riposte. It is achieved by immediate recovery after a main attack and the launch of a new attack to score.

LEARNING EXPERIENCE—THE REDOUBLEMENT

With absence of the blades, middle distance.
Fencer A: Attack with lunge.
Fencer B: Retreat.
Fencer A: Recover forward, lunge, and score.

The Stop Thrust

The stop thrust is a counteroffensive action that is successful against the opponent's compound or indecisive attack. It is executed by scoring as the opponent initiates a compound attack, attempts to take the blade, or hesitates.

In order to succeed, the stop thrust must arrive before the attacker has begun the final movement of the attack. If the stop thrust is used against a simple attack, and if both arrive, the counterattacker will be declared hit—even if the stop thrust landed first.

To execute the stop thrust properly, the fencer must choose the right moment to launch the counterattack, then follow through without hesitation and without giving away the intent. When there is doubt about whether the original attack or the stop thrust has the right-of-way, the decision will generally be in favor of the original attack.

Stop Thrust

The Action of Second Intention

The action of second intention is a false offensive or defensive movement to lure the opponent into a committed reaction. The fencer convinces the opponent that he or she can score with the stop thrust by pretending that a compound attack or an attempt to take opponent's blade is planned. Having lured the adversary into a counterattack, the fencer defends oneself while executing a false attack, and scores in second intention (counter-time).

The fencer who parries the opponent's riposte and scores with a counter-riposte may also be executing a second intention. Convincing the opponent that the initial action is real requires a sense of timing and distance, strong defense, and a quick offense on the part of the fencer.

Counter Riposte in
Lunge Position

LEARNING EXPERIENCE—SECOND INTENTION

1. *Engage the blades in 6th position, middle distance.*
   Fencer A: Attack indirectly into the inside line with a short lunge.
   Fencer B: Parry 4 and riposte.
   Fencer A: In lunge position, parry 4 and score with counter-riposte.
2. *Engage in 6th, long distance.*
   Fencer A: Attempt to change engagement into 4th with advance.
   Fencer B: Counterattack into outside high line with extension.
   Fencer A: Parry 6 and score indirectly with lunge (counter-time).

Remise, riposte, and redoublement may also be executed as actions of second intention.

HIGHLIGHTS

1. Explain how to relate and adapt new skills and techniques to your game.
2. Demonstrate a low-line attack on another fencer.
3. Name and demonstrate the two semicircular or low-line parries.
4. Demonstrate that you know how to execute each compound attack.
5. Define a compound riposte and demonstrate one type.
6. Explain and demonstrate what is meant by a renewed attack and give three examples of such attacks.
7. Explain what is meant by "taking the blade."
8. Compare and contrast verbally and by demonstration the different kinds of transfers.
9. Describe and show the action of second intention.
10. With an opponent, demonstrate the proper timing and tempo for executing a stop thrust.
11. Explain and demonstrate the difference between a balestra and an advance-lunge.
12. Explain the precautions a fencer must take in executing a flèche attack.

3

Saber

INTRODUCTION

Those who are uninitiated to the sport of fencing may think it too complicated and difficult for anyone to become competent in any of the three weapons. But fencing is no more difficult to learn than any other sport, and those who have participated in it will testify to the lifelong benefits they derived from it.

This chapter is a basic introduction to saber fencing. The development of elite saber fencers requires several years of training. In this chapter, we cover the aspects of saber training normally introduced in the first and second years. We assume that the student has had some preparatory fencing education. Basic concepts, preliminary movements, actions, and drills that form the foundation for advanced learning are covered.

All fencing actions must be mastered from all distances with various combinations of footwork. Footwork is of paramount importance, regardless of the weapon used. Footwork is a relatively easy fencing skill to master because it is perfected through rote learning. To develop superior footwork, the fencer must practice the footwork skills—and their variations and combinations—with great frequency at increasingly higher rates of speed and intensity.

We are not implying that footwork must be taught before bladework. To the contrary, all elements of the sport should be introduced during the initial stages of instruction, so that the student can integrate all elements of fencing into his or her bouting and put together an effective fencing style. The learning fencer should spend a great deal of time developing speed, strength, agility, endurance, and sense of balance. As the fencer's body grows stronger and balance and mobility improve, the technical execution will also improve. These enhanced physical qualities will make it possible to develop a strong, powerful fighting game and the ability to apply any necessary tactics and strategy.

The fencing coach or instructor teaches fencing movements and actions, encourages and motivates, and provides an environment for students to practice and perfect fencing skills. It is the student's responsibility to continue to practice these movements.

When learning a movement, the student should first execute it perfectly at a low rate of speed. Then the speed may be gradually increased until maximum speed and coordination are achieved in the full range of motion. This is true for every fencing action or combination of actions. The simple fact is that *the only way to perfect a movement is to practice it extensively and consistently.*

THE DEVELOPMENT OF SABER FENCING

Modern saber fencing originated in Italy, where in 1878 three fencing academies were established: one in Modena, one in Parma, and one in Milan. Their objectives were to train fencing masters for the army.

Giuseppe Radaelli, in charge of the school in Milan, was given the responsibility of developing saber fencing. His most important contribution to today's sport was his teaching technique that the elbow should be the axis for leading and directing the saber actions. Control of the weapon with the forearm with as little wrist movement as possible is retained even today and dominates the technique of the elite fencers in the world. About the end of the nineteenth century, the light Italian saber was introduced. This led to the development of the modern competitive weapon.

Hungarian fencers, utilizing the Italian style of fencing, further simplified the movements, which became more effective, as proven by the development of Hungarian international champions for over half a century. In the latter half of the twentieth century, the Soviet Union, Poland, and other Eastern European countries have dominated international tournaments in saber.

WEAPON AND EQUIPMENT FOR SABER FENCING

Saber, glove, jacket, electrical jacket, mask, knickers, body cord, shoes, and socks are equipment needed for saber fencing. Knowing how to select, care for, and maintain the equipment is very important.

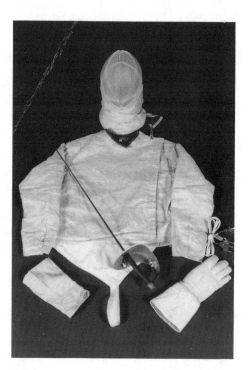

The Saber

The saber is a cutting and thrusting weapon composed of a blade, a guard, a handle, and a pommel.

The *blade,* approximately rectangular in section, has a theoretical cutting edge and a back edge. The end of the blade is folded over itself to form a blunt tip, which is square or rectangular with a cross section of 4 millimeters minimum and 6 millimeters maximum. The fold of the blunt tip must not close more than 3 millimeters from the end of the blade.

The blade is theoretically divided into four parts. The *tang* is the part which is inserted into the handle. Nearest to the guard is the *forté* (strong part). The center part is called the *middle*. The top one-third of the blade near the tip is called the *foible* (the weak part).

By regulation, blades that are too rigid or too whippy are forbidden. Blades may have a curve, but the curve must be continuous and its deflection must be less than 4 centimeters. The length of a blade may not exceed 88 centimeters. The total length of a saber may not exceed 105 centimeters. Its total weight usually is less than 500 grams. Regulations concerning the dimensions and characteristics of the nonelectric saber are equally valid—without any change—for the electric saber.

The *guard,* made from either steel or aluminum, must have a continuous convex form in one piece, with a smooth external surface without rim or holes. It must be

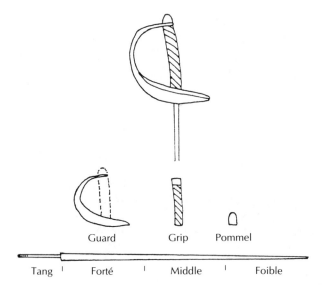

Guard   Grip   Pommel

Tang   Forté   Middle   Foible

Parts of the Saber

able to pass through a rectangular gauge measuring 15 centimeters by 14 centimeters in cross section, with a length of 15 centimeters.

Inside the guard for an electrical saber there must be two connectors: one in which to plug the body cord, and the other for mounting the sensor. By regulation, the mounting for the sensor (accelerometer) must be affixed inside the guard and attached firmly to the guard itself. To this mounting there must be attached a four-pin ARCHER (TANDY) socket (Type 274001) or a BNC socket. The four pins must be connected to the blade, the guard, the body cord socket, and the sensor.

The interior of the guard for an electrical saber must be completely insulated by an insulating finish or pad. The exterior of the guard must be insulated 7 to 8 centimeters from the pommel. The handle and the pommel must be completely insulated. The guard must be electrically insulated from the blade. The insulation between the projection from the guard should not be more than 0.5 centimeters and will not be considered part of the length of the blade.

The saber *hilt* is made like a handle and holds the tang of the blade and a pommel (the rear portion of the hilt) that locks the handle into the tang.

The Glove

The glove is essential for safety. (See Chapter 1 for additional information.) For electrical saber competitions, by regulation the glove on the weapon arm must also be covered by a metallic fabric on the back of the hand as far as the fingers and over the entire cuff. To guarantee effective contact with the sleeve of the metallic jacket, it is necessary to use an elastic band, a snap, or any approved system capable of ensuring contact.

The Jacket

A safe jacket is one that provides ample protection. (See Chapter 1 for additional information.) In electrical saber fencing, by regulation, the fencer must wear a *metallic jacket* over the fencing jacket, and the metallic surface must cover the entire valid surface area of the body (the target area).

The sleeves of the metallic jacket must be fixed at the wrists by an elastic band, and a strap must pass between the legs of the fencer to hold the jacket in place. In the middle of the back, beneath the collar, the metallic jacket must have a 2-by-3 centimeter metallic tab for attaching the mask wire with a crocodile clip.

The Mask

Safety considerations require a mask. (See Chapter 1 for additional information.) In electric saber fencing, the mesh of the mask must not be insulated. The bib and any trim must be entirely covered by a metallic material that has the same electrical characteristics as the metallic jacket. The electrical resistance between the crocodile clip, which is attached to the metallic jacket, and every part of the mask must be less than 3 ohms. Electrical contact between the metallic jacket and the mask must be secured by a wire (30–40 centimeters long), with two soldered crocodile clips—one for the mask and one for the electric jacket.

Knickers, Shoes, and Socks

Knickers and knee socks are required for protection. Shoes must have rubber soles for good traction and comfort.

The Body Cord

A body cord is essential for electrical saber fencing. Fencers must use an insulated body cord that is worn inside the sleeve of the weapon arm and extends down the back beneath the jacket. One end of the cord is connected to the socket in the guard; the other end is plugged into a spring-loaded reel. The clip on the body cord is the end that is attached to the metallic jacket.

Selecting Equipment

Guidelines for selecting fencing equipment are in Chapter 1.

HIGHLIGHTS

1. Identify the parts of a saber.
2. Explain why a new saber blade should be bent, in what direction, and how it should be done.
3. Identify the parts of a saber blade.
4. State the function of a pommel.
5. Describe the saber mask for electrical competition.
6. Describe how a mask and an electrical jacket are attached to ensure conductivity.
7. Describe a regulation glove for electrical saber competition.

BASIC SKILLS

Mastering basic skills is a prerequisite to efficient performance.

The Basic and On-Guard Positions

The basic and on-guard positions for foil fencing, which are almost the same for saber and épée too (with some slight modifications), are described in Chapter 1.

In the saber on-guard position, however, the shoulders and the trunk are turned toward the opponent at approximately 30–45 degrees from the bout plane, compared with 20–30 degrees for foil. The rear arm is bent slightly and rests next to the trailing hip. The weapon arm is placed a little closer to the trunk than in the foil position.

Footwork

The footwork for saber is the same as for foil, but in saber fencing the stance is more erect, the center of gravity in the lunge position is higher, and the lunge itself is shorter. Saber fencers use the cross-step, the balestra, and the flèche more often, as well as a greater variety of compound footwork.

The Cross-Advance and Cross-Retreat

To execute a cross-advance, shift the body weight by crossing the rear foot in front of the leading foot. At the same time, transfer the body's weight to the rear foot and move the leading foot forward to the on-guard position. This permits the center of gravity to be evenly distributed on both legs.

Try to do a cross-retreat using the same principle.

Cross Advance

Distance and Timing

See Chapter 2, on foil fencing.

The Saber Grip

Grasping the saber handle properly is an important skill that is a key to developing effective offensive and defensive maneuvers with the blade.

Saber Handle Grasp

To grip the saber handle properly, grasp the handle of the saber 1 centimeter behind the guard. Grip the saber with the thumb on top of the handle and the first phalanx of the index finger on the bottom. The pommel extends beyond and below the hand. The little finger holds the handle against the cushion of the palm. The other two fingers are lightly placed on the handle. There should be a space between the handle and the interior of the palm. The handle does not touch the palm's interior. The saber is held in a relaxed manner.

Avoid the following mistakes:

Holding the grip too tightly.
Holding the handle against the interior of the palm.
Holding the grip at the end of the handle (by the pommel).
Holding the saber along the forearm as if it were a foil.

LEARNING EXPERIENCE—THE GRIP

1. *Grip a pencil or rolled piece of paper the way you would grip the saber handle.*
2. *Grip the object only with the manipulators (thumb and index fingers).*
3. *Relax and press the imaginary saber handle several times. Do you feel the blade moving down when you press the object, and the blade moving up as you relax?*

The Salute

Historically the salute is the fencer's acknowledgment of one's worthy opponent and the code of sportsmanlike conduct that is expected to be exercised as a standard throughout the combat. The salute, although brief and brisk, remains today as a symbol of courtesy, goodwill, and sportsmanship. See Chapter 2 on Foil Fencing for description of salute.

The Salute

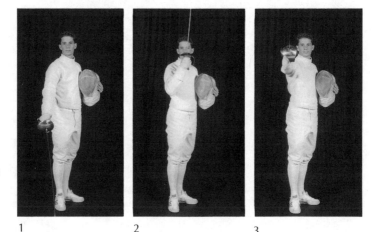

1   2   3

1. Demonstrate the proper way to grip a saber.
2. Holding the mask in the nonweapon hand, assume the position of attention and execute a salute with the saber. Explain the purpose of the salute.
3. With hands on hips, demonstrate the on-guard position of the legs.
4. With hands on hips, demonstrate the advance and the retreat.
5. With hands on hips, demonstrate the lunge and recovery.
6. Describe the bout (fencing) line.
7. With hands on hips, demonstrate a cross-step forward and backward.

Fundamental Hand Positions and Change of Position

It is important to know (1) how to position the weapon hand correctly, (2) how to ensure the protection of specific target areas, (3) how to define the exact placement of the saber in the guard positions and parries, and (4) how to execute cuts and thrusts accurately.

Note: Though 1st and 2nd positions are described below, this book emphasizes 3rd, 4th, and 5th positions.

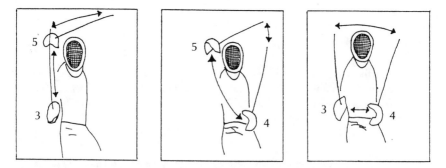

Weapon Positions and Change of Positions

1st Position

First position protects the chest and belly from an attack to the lower inside line. The hand is overpronated with the saber point below the guard. The cutting edge of the blade is placed to absorb the opponent's cut.

2nd Position

Second position protects the flank and the forearm from an attack to the low outside line. The hand is overpronated, and the blade and forearm are in a straight line. The cutting edge faces outward, with the point below the guard and directed forward and down.

1st Position

2nd Position

3rd Position

Third position protects the flank, the outside target area (including the hand, the forearm, and the cheek), and the parts of the outside target nearest to the opponent. It usually serves as the on-guard position.

The upper arm and forearm should be relaxed and placed in the fencing plane. The forearm is normally parallel to the floor. The hand is turned to the outside of the fencing line with the palm facing generally forward and downward. If this is done properly, the cutting edge of the saber will now be turned outside, 30 to 45 degrees from the bout plane. The thumb is placed behind the cutting edge to absorb the impact of the opponent's cut. The point of the saber is directed forward and inward toward the opponent's left eye.

3rd Position

LEARNING EXPERIENCE—3RD POSITION

1. *Using a full-length mirror, look at your image as you assume the on-guard position in 3rd and imagine it to be your opponent. With the thumbnail facing directly upward (12 o'clock), extend the sword arm straight ahead until the point touches the top of the mask seen in the mirror.*
2. *From this extended position, simultaneously turn your wrist to the right so the thumb is pointed toward a 2 o'clock position. Maintain the point at eye level, and lower the elbow toward your waistline, stopping before it is a fist's length from the hip.*
3. *Position the guard slightly below the waistline and to the outside of the fencing plane. Keep the shoulders level, and the back, spine, and head erect.*
4. *Position the forearm in the bout plane, slightly downward and almost parallel to the floor.*
5. *Check to see whether your on-guard position is now similar to that shown in the illustration.*
6. *Have an instructor or partner "cut" lightly on your guard to check the correctness of your on-guard position.*

4th Position

Fourth position protects the inside high line. This includes the chest, the belly, and the inside target area—hand, forearm, and cheek. The guard is placed forward of the body and in front of the left side of the torso, slightly below the waistline. The shoulders remain relaxed, with the upper arm in the fencing line. The thumb and

4th Position

forearm are approximately in the same plane. In this position, a line that runs through the forearm, the thumb, and the cutting edge forms an angle of 45 to 60 degrees from the bout line.

LEARNING EXPERIENCE—4TH POSITION

1. *From the on-guard position, extend the arm in the fencing line, rest the cutting edge on the top of the mask of a partner or mannequin.*
2. *From this extended position, simultaneously flex the wrist inward (do not rotate the fingers) and collapse the elbow toward the waistline.*
3. *The elbow should be positioned at least one fist span from the hip.*
4. *Repeat this exercise many times with a partner, a mannequin, and in front of a mirror.*

Avoid the following mistakes:

Moving the guard beyond the inside (4th) line, too far from the body.
Positioning the guard too high or too low.
Flexing the wrist incorrectly or too far, so the thumb is unable to absorb the cut.
Allowing the point to drop and expose the upper part of the target.

3rd to 4th Position

Changing from 3rd Position to 4th

After repeating 4th position many times, with the instructor or partner correcting the principal errors, you can move on to learn to move from 3rd position to 4th.

To move from 3rd to 4th position, flex the wrist (do not rotate the fingers) to the left and move the guard with the forearm, using the elbow as a stationary pivot from the outside line (from the right) to the inside line (to the left).

The movement from 4th to 3rd position starts with flexing the wrist to the right. It is important that at the end of the movement the edge of the blade is turned to meet the opponent's cut directly, with the thumb positioned in passive support. The rest is as described above.

Avoid the following mistakes:

Turning the guard too late—that is, after the forearm has moved.
Rotating the fingers on the handle.
Making the movements too large.

LEARNING EXPERIENCE—CHANGE OF POSITIONS, 3RD–4TH–3RD

1. *In front of the mirror, at a very slow pace and holding a pencil as you would a saber, move from 3rd position to 4th. Make sure to flex the wrist first, allowing the thumb and the cutting edge of the blade to absorb the cut.*
2. *Repeat the action from 4th position to 3rd.*
3. *Perform this change with retreat. (This action should be initiated with the movement of the rear foot as the fencer retreats.)*
4. *Change position with advance. (This action should be initiated with the movement of the leading foot as the fencer advances.)*
5. *Perform a double change of position, 3rd–4th–3rd. First, while retreating: As the rear foot moves, make the first change; as the front foot moves, make the second change. Then with advance: The first change is done with the leading foot advancing; the second change is done with the trailing foot completing the advance.*

5th Position

5th Position

Fifth position protects the head and the upper limits of the target area. In this position, the shoulder should be relaxed, the forearm almost vertical and placed in the bout plane; the elbow should stop at shoulder level, the wrist at head level; the palm should be turned forward. The edge of the blade faces upward. The blade is placed almost horizontally, with the point slightly above your head. Hold the point slightly forward toward the opponent.

Avoid the following mistakes:

Moving the elbow outside of the bout plane.
Moving the guard inside or outside of the bout plane.
Leaving the point below the horizontal plane.
Placing the guard above the shoulder but not high enough to protect the head.

LEARNING EXPERIENCE—5TH POSITION

1. *From 3rd position, lower the point of the saber to the left until it almost reaches a horizontal position. Now the forearm should be nearly parallel to the floor and remains in the bout plane.*
2. *Keeping the shoulder relaxed, raise the saber just above your head until the elbow reaches shoulder level.*
3. *While keeping the movements small, repeat the movement from on-guard to 5th position several times in front of the mirror.*
4. *Stand by a wall near a door, your right side (for right-handed fencers) as close to*

the wall as possible, with only your wrist and saber protruding past the door opening. Slowly raise your hand from on-guard (3rd) to 5th position and back, checking that the elbow does not touch the wall. Execute all movements smoothly.

5.   *Practice this change with the advance and retreat.*

Basic Saber Cuts and Thrusts

Head Cut

The head cut is executed by a single uninterrupted movement of the hand accelerating toward the moment of the cut.

Note: From the on-guard position in 3rd, the flexing of the wrist, not the fingers, should direct the cutting edge of the blade toward the opponent's head at the start of the extension.

After flexing, the cutting edge should move forward directly to the head. To execute the final motion of the cut, the thumb should push forward supported by the contraction of the little finger pressing the weapon handle against the pad of the palm. In the final position, the arm should be fully extended, without locking the elbow joint! With the guard at shoulder level, the cutting edge should be directed forward and downward.

The hit should not be pushed or delivered stiffly. After the hit arrives, the arm

The Head Cut

should relax and remain almost fully extended—that is, avoid locking the elbow joint in the cutting position.

It is useful to remain in the cut position for a moment without returning the arm to the on-guard position immediately. From this position, the fencer may pursue other options.

LEARNING EXPERIENCE—THE HEAD CUT

1. *In 3rd position, standing close to your partner, flex your wrist toward the target (the opponent's head) and cut with almost no extension. Make certain that the edge of the blade contacts the target directly or perpendicular to the target surface. Repeat the action several times before returning to the on-guard position.*
2. *Increase the distance a little. With half-extension, execute single, then double, head cuts, following the same principle as in #1.*
3. *Further extending the distance, execute single and double head cuts with full extension. Pay close attention to the quality of the movement. Return slowly to the on-guard position.*
4. *Practice the head cut with half-advance and half-lunge.*

Head Cut from 4th Position

While executing a head cut from 4th position, the fencer *need not make a conscious effort to turn the guard during the movement* toward the target. The guard will

Parry 4

automatically turn while the arm is extending toward the target. The final positions of the arm, the guard, and the blade should be the same as in the head cut from 3rd position. Repeat this cut many times with a partner, a mannequin, and in front of a mirror.

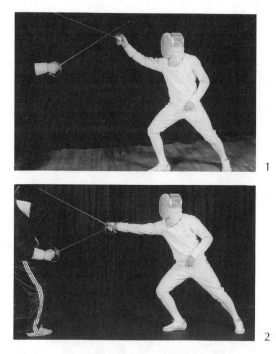

Head Cut from 5th Position

1

2

Head Cut from 5th Position

To execute this cut, the fencer must rotate the wrist and pivot the point backward around and above the head until it reaches the fencing plane, with the cutting edge directed upward-forward. Then the fencer begins the cutting motion, delivering the blade forward to the opponent's head in the bout plane. After learning the sequence of these movements, execute the cut without hesitation.

LEARNING EXPERIENCE—HEAD CUT FROM 4TH AND 5TH POSITIONS

1. *From a closer short distance, execute single and double head cuts from 4th and 5th positions with no extension, as described above. Repeat the action several times before returning to on-guard.*
2. *Practice the head cut with half-extension, first from 4th position and then from 5th.*

3. *Execute the head cut with full extension in the same manner as in #1 and #2 above. Pay close attention to the quality of the movement. Slowly return to on-guard.*

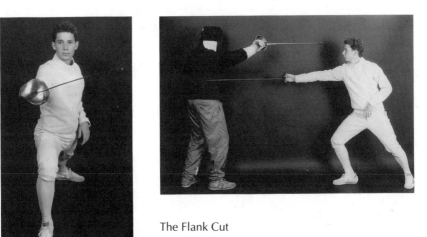

The Flank Cut

The Flank Cut

From the 3rd position, the flank cut is executed by delivering the cutting edge of the blade to the side of the body, using the fingers in the same way as the head cut. The fencer learns the flank cut in two stages:

1. Simultaneously rotate the wrist to pronate the hand, and turn the blade in the horizontal plane so that the cutting edge/guard is turned slightly upward.
2. Deliver the final cut keeping the wrist/guard in the bout plane.

The hand reaches full pronation while moving forward to the target. The cutting edge is delivered to the target with the cut executed primarily by the arm extension, supported by a slight fingers-wrist movement. (The guard stays a little below shoulder level in the final position.) Avoid locking the elbow joint.

Recovery: The arm returns to the on-guard position by flexing the elbow. At the same time, the wrist pulls the blade back, circling it in an upward and forward motion and returning to a perfect on-guard position.

Avoid the following mistakes:

Positioning the guard inside of the bout plane at the cut position.
· Placing the point above or below the horizontal plane during the delivery of the blade to the target.

Turning the cutting edge away from the target during the delivery of the blade to the target, causing the cut to land flat.
Recovering the weapon arm too quickly.
Lifting the guard above shoulder level.

LEARNING EXPERIENCE—THE FLANK CUT

1. *Partner in 5th position, standing close. The fencer should slowly pronate the hand and rotate the forearm to cut to the flank with minimal extension.*
2. *Same action as #1, with full extension from short distance.*
3. *Same action as #1, with half-lunge. First provide direction to the sabre; follow with the half-lunge. Simultaneously with the leg movement, complete the extension and score.*

Focus your attention on:

Avoiding touching your partner's elbow while delivering the flank-cut.
Having your thumb execute the cut.
Recovering slowly.
Developing a sensitivity for the correct saber grip.

The technique of the flank cut from 4th position is similar to the technique from 3rd position.

The Chest Cut

The chest cut is very similar to the head cut, except the wrist is rotated so the hand is turned toward supination. The blade lands on the opponent's upper chest or left

The Chest Cut

shoulder, for a right-handed fencer. The belly cut is technically more difficult and less practical than the chest cut, so we shall focus on the chest cut here.

The Chest Cut

LEARNING EXPERIENCE—THE CHEST CUT

1. *From a very* short distance *in the on-guard position, turn the cutting edge toward your partner's trailing shoulder and, using your wrist-fingers alone, execute the cut without extension. Recover slowly to 3rd position.*
2. *From* short distance, *turn the cutting edge toward your partner's trailing shoulder. Start the motion slowly. While accelerating the extension of the arm, activate the wrist-fingers for the cut. Recover slowly.*
3. *Repeat 35–40 times with your partner and in front of the mirror. Be sure that the beginning of cut is performed without elevating the wrist.*

The Point Thrust

The saber is primarily a cutting weapon, but point actions are frequently used. The *direct thrust* is executed from 3rd position by lowering the point toward the chest, fully pronating the hand, extending the arm to hit, and bringing the guard in line with the shoulder.

Thrust with
Opposition

Thrust with Lunge

LEARNING EXPERIENCE—THE POINT THRUST

Direct Thrust:
1. *From a very short distance: Assume the on-guard position. Execute the straight thrust with slight extension very slowly.*
2. *From short distance: Lower the point, then deliver the thrust with full extension.*
3. *From middle distance: Repeat the same action as in #2 with a lunge, paying attention to the smoothness of the movements:*
   a. *Lowering the point.*
   b. *Extending the arm.*
   c. *Following through with the lunge. Recover slowly.*

Indirect Thrust, short distance, from engagement in 3rd position:
1. *Bring the point of the saber into the line by rotating the wrist so the hand is*

in a fully pronated position. Avoid contacting the opponent's guard with your point.

2. *Extend your arm to touch opponent's chest with your point. The hand is held at shoulder level, with the guard rim turned to the outside.*

Ultimately, the point thrust should be executed by one uninterrupted extension of the arm, delivering the point to the target. To recover, the arm returns along the fencing plane by bending the elbow and simultaneously using the fingers and wrist to return the blade to the on-guard position.

Avoid the following mistakes:

Extending the arm before giving direction to the point.
Holding the hand too high or too low, or displacing it too far to the outside.
Not turning the cutting edge of the saber to the outside.
Recovering the arm to on-guard with a hard or jerky motion.
Allowing the wrist to be above or below the shoulder.

Attacks from Different Distances

Attacks from Middle Distance

Having practiced the cuts from short distance, you are ready to learn attacks from middle distance. The attack with lunge is executed with the arm accelerating in the final moment of the cut. The cut may precede or coincide with the landing of the leading foot.

It is possible to develop the technique to the point where one is able to cut before the leading foot lands, but it requires years of practice. Therefore, start the delivery of the blade only slightly before, or at the same time as, the action of the front foot.

LEARNING EXPERIENCE—ATTACK FROM MIDDLE DISTANCE

From a shorter middle distance:

1. *Rotate the cutting edge of the blade toward the opponent's target without fully extending. Do not attempt to cut. Do the same with a half-advance, as a preparation to a lunge. Occasionally attack with a lunge.*
2. *Attack the head with a lunge. Remain in the final lunge position; check the position of the cut (arm, wrist, hand, blade). Recover the arm only. Repeat the cut several times while still in the lunge position. Make sure your arm recovers smoothly to 3rd position each time. Recover to on-guard.*
3. *Try alternative coordination schemes. Attack to the head with an advance. As the leading foot moves forward, keep your hand protected in 3rd position. After your leading foot lands, launch a cut as the rear foot concludes its motion. The cut should be immediate and direct, arriving with the landing of the rear foot.*

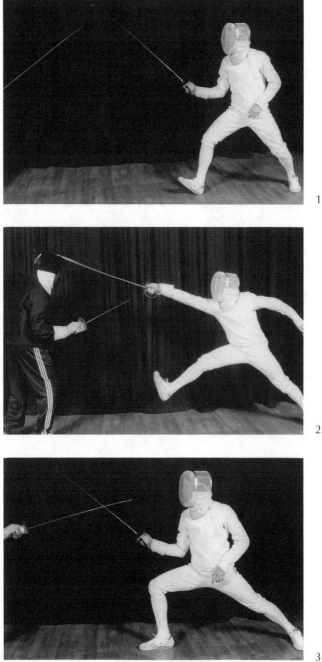

1

2

3

From longer distance:

Attack to the head on the opponent's advance: (1) Hold your ground while your partner advances and retreats. Attack with lunge into one of the opponent's advances. (2) As your partner advances and retreats, maintain proper distance. Attack with lunge into one of partner's advances.

Avoid the following mistakes:

Overextending the lunge, which results in the center of gravity being too low, making it difficult to execute the next action in time.

Positioning the arm out of line with the shoulder, turning the guard away from the target.

Extending the arm too early—that is, from a distance too far from the target, making one subject to stop-cut in time.

Extending the arm too late—that is, from a distance too close to the target, making one subject to counterattack to the head or with the point.

Lunge Position

Attack from Long Distance

When attacking from long distance, the fencer most commonly uses an advance-lunge or balestra (jump forward–lunge). These attacks should first be learned in slow motion. As the fencer's skill improves, the speed of an attack should increase. The beginning of the advance is slower and smoother, then the attack accelerates as the rear foot completes its step and the leading foot thrusts forward.

The cutting motion begins only when the fencer is able to reach the target with one uninterrupted movement.

Upon completion of an attack, the final position (lunge) should be held for a short time before recovering to on-guard. This is vital for making a proper, balanced recovery after each attack. Once in a while, however, the fencer should learn to recover quickly after an attack as a starting point from which to expand his or her repertoire—for example, when the fencer recovers immediately after an unsuccessful attack to avoid being hit by the riposte.

LEARNING EXPERIENCE—ATTACK FROM LONG DISTANCE

1. Execute an attack with balestra against a mannequin.
2. Attack to partner's open target with advance-lunge.
3. Have a partner slowly change hand positions. Choosing the correct moment, attack the opening target with an advance-lunge.
4. Attack a partner with a balestra, and score before he or she can retreat.
5. Lead your partner by advancing and retreating while he or she maintains the distance. Choose the moment after your advance to attack with balestra when the partner hesitates to move.
6. Lead as in #5. Choose the moment for an attack with a lunge into your partner's advance after you have executed a half-retreat.

Avoid the following mistakes:

Shifting the center of gravity too far forward during the advance, causing the rear foot to move too close to the leading foot.

Extending the weapon arm too soon in the advance (it becomes an easy target for the opponent's stop-cut).

Extending the weapon arm too late, giving the opponent an opportunity to counter-attack into the preparation.

HIGHLIGHTS

1. From 3rd position, demonstrate the proper way to execute a direct thrust with the point to the chest.
2. From 4th position, demonstrate a head cut from middle distance.
3. From 5th position, demonstrate a head cut from short distance.
4. From 3rd position, demonstrate an attack to the chest from middle distance, and recover.
5. From 3rd position, describe the execution and coordination of the foot and arm movements for a head cut from long distance and the recovery.
6. List three mistakes or errors to avoid in attacking from middle distance to the head, flank, or chest.

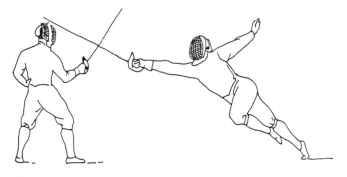

The Flèche Attack

The Flèche Attack*

A good fencer uses every possible method of footwork to establish a rich and varied game, and the flèche attack is an integral part of saber fencing. The flèche is also the only movement in fencing that is more or less natural, but it is important to execute it perfectly.

The flèche attack is executed in one fencing time. The action starts with the slight shifting of the center of gravity forward, ahead of the leading foot. Then, while reaching with the sword arm in a continually accelerating motion, the fencer forcefully pushes off with the leading foot, propelling the body forward.

From the tip of the saber to the toes of the leading foot, the fencer stretches in one straight line with one goal—to reach out and touch the target!

The rear foot is actively swung forward, carrying the weight of the body as the fencer completes the flèche by running past the opponent's unarmed side.

Landing After Successful Flèche

*At press time, the FIE was investigating ways to make saber competitions simpler and more understandable for the general public. One option is to eliminate the use of flèches and cross-advances.

The flèche is sometimes preceded by a running preparation, executed by actually running at the opponent or taking a series of cross-steps ending with the flèche. The most common error in executing the running attack is getting too close to the opponent and cutting late.

The flèche attack can be executed from the on-guard position; from the advance or retreat, the half-advance, the half-lunge, or the half-retreat; from the jump forward or backward; after the cross-advance or cross-retreat; and as a redoublement from the lunge position.

LEARNING EXPERIENCE—FLÈCHE ATTACK

1. *From short distance, execute a head cut in one uninterrupted arm movement.*
2. *From a slightly longer distance, execute a head cut by leaning forward while shifting the center of gravity toward the opponent.*
3. *From an increasingly longer distance, execute a head cut by actually losing balance forward. Conclude by bringing the back leg across the leading leg to reestablish balance.*

Note: Leaning forward with your leading knee bent helps maintain the proper direction of the flèche attack.

4. *From long distance, your partner is advancing and retreating while you hold your ground. Choose the right moment to attack with a flèche into one of the advances.*
5. *Attack with half-advance, flèche against a motionless opponent.*
6. *Attack with advance—half-lunge—flèche against a retreating opponent.*
7. *Repeat the flèche attack exercises above, incorporating a chest cut, a flank cut, or a point-thrust action.*

Avoid the following mistakes:

Leaning forward before you are close enough to reach the opponent, thus giving away your intention to attack.

Falling after the flèche, usually the result of your rear leg stepping short and therefore being of no help in retaining the balance.

Jumping vertically in the flèche, usually caused by keeping the leading knee locked. Keep the leading knee bent like a spring.

Running aside from the opponent while flèching (fearing a collision). Have courage. You soon will learn to avoid a collision without sacrificing speed.

HIGHLIGHTS

1. What is a flèche?
2. Describe the execution of a flèche.
3. List three positions from which the flèche can be started.

4.   What causes a fencer to move vertically when attacking with a flèche?
5.   How does a fencer give away his or her intention to execute the flèche?

Attack to the Open Target

The ability to recognize an open target area and to execute an *attack-in-time* is one of the most important skills for a fencer to learn. When recognizing the open target, the attack-in-time requires correct execution of the simple attack. It should be performed in a single action. The element of surprise increases the chance of successfully scoring.

LEARNING EXPERIENCE—ATTACK TO THE OPEN TARGET

From middle distance:
1.   *While your partner slowly moves the saber from the 5th to low (2nd) position and then back to 5th, choose the correct moment to attack the head (or flank) with a timely lunge while the opponent changes position.*
2.   *Using the same concept as in #1, your partner slowly moves his or her saber between 3rd and 4th positions. Your task now is to attack against the change to the flank (or chest).*

From short distance:
3.   *Your partner slowly changes guard positions as in #1 above. Choose the correct moment to make a timely cut to the opening target and, as your partner continues moving from one position to another, cut at another opening target. Then slowly recover to on-guard. The same drill can be done from the middle distance, where your attack is executed with a lunge and the second cut is done while you remain in lunge position.*

From middle distance:
4.   *As your partner moves forward, he or she assumes 5th position; when retreating, 3rd position. Hold your ground and, at the proper moment, cut to your partner's flank with an extension when he or she advances, or attack with a lunge or flèche to the head when your partner retreats.*
5.   *Repeat the drill in #4. Have your partner randomly change hand positions. The task is to cut with an arm extension only to the opening target as the partner advances, or to attack with lunge or flèche and cut to the opening target as the opponent retreats.*

Beat Attack

The beat attack brings variety and an element of surprise to a bout. It distracts the opponent's attention and reduces his or her ability to act effectively.

Beats can be executed with either the cutting edge or the back edge of the blade. The beat should be a crisp, light action that stops at the point of contact. Beat actions can be direct, semicircular, circular, or grazing.

All attacks utilizing the beat can be executed against all target areas. In the initial learning stages one should use the cutting edge of the blade for practicing the *beat attack to the head*. This technique is structurally simple, easy to comprehend, and useful to employ in the bout.

Before executing this or any other beat attack from long distance, learn to execute it from short and medium distance, as in the accompanying Learning Experience.

The Beat in 4

LEARNING EXPERIENCE—THE BEAT ATTACK

From short distance:
1. *With both fencers in 3rd position and no weapon engagement, beat your opponent's blade toward your 4th line (beat 4) with the cutting edge of the blade (the thumb behind the cutting edge). Pause, check to be sure the position of the blade is correct and the arm is moved slightly forward. Then proceed with acceleration, cut to the mask. Pause and slowly recover.*
2. *Reverse roles and have your partner practice the same action.*
3. *When both fencers have learned to execute the action properly, reduce the length of the pauses between the beat and the cut until the action becomes an*

uninterrupted, flowing movement. Try the following: Beat 4 cut forearm, cut shoulder, cut head. Start slowly, then accelerate.

From middle distance:

4.   Take the same hand position as in #1. Execute a light beat 4 with a small arm movement forward, pause to check your position, then proceed to the attack with the lunge in a single uninterrupted motion. Pause again in the lunge position, then slowly recover to on-guard.

5.   Reverse roles and have your partner practice the same.

6.   *Practice the following: Beat 4; with half extension cut to the forearm; check the position, then with a lunge attack to the head.*

From long distance:

7.   *Assume the same hand position as in #1. Maintain your hand in 3rd position as you begin the advance with your leading foot. At the moment when the rear foot concludes the advance, execute a beat 4 by slightly extending the weapon arm. At this point you should be in the same position as in #1—so lunge!*

8.   *While you hold the saber pointed downward in 2nd position, your partner leads you by advancing and retreating. At random, just before advancing, your partner lifts his or her weapon in an extended 3rd position. This should be the moment for you to start a beat 4 flèche attack to the head, instead of retreating. Should your partner lift his or her blade while retreating, launch a beat attack with a half-lunge–flèche to the head.*

9.   *You lead. Your partner, in an extended 3rd position, maintains the distance from you. Carefully choose the moment to execute a beat attack with lunge, an advance lunge, or a flèche, according to the length of the distance between you and your opponent at different moments in your opponent's footwork.*

10. *Once again reverse roles and allow your partner to practice the same as in #4 and #5.*

Parry and Riposte

A basic parry (blocking parry) protects the target area by placing the weapon on defense in a split moment prior to receiving an opponent's cut or thrust. This is accomplished with a short, controlled movement of the weapon.

Parries taken by the cutting edge of the blade (thumb behind the cutting edge) give the fencer a proper tactile feeling. At first, the fencer learns parry and riposte from the stationary guard position. Later, the skill is developed enough to be executed while retreating and advancing.

The steps in the progressive learning and development of the parry-riposte skill are as follows:

1.   Preplan the entire action, parry and riposte.

2.   Choose an appropriate parry; score with the preplanned riposte.

3.   Preplan the parry; choose an appropriate riposte.

LEARNING EXPERIENCE—PARRY AND RIPOSTE

Parry 3, Riposte to the head:

1. *From short distance, you are in 3rd position. Your partner deliberately cuts into your blade. Execute a head cut as soon as the impact is felt. After a pause, slowly relax the weapon arm to on-guard.*
2. *You are in 4th position. Your partner attacks to the flank with varying speeds. Take parry 3 and riposte to your partner's head.*
3. *From middle distance, you are in a half-extension with the cutting edge of the saber turned toward the opponent's head, a half-feint. (The half-feint position gives the defender certain advantages: increased distance between the saber and the body allows a fencer more time and space for making defensive or counter-offensive decisions.) Your partner attacks the flank slowly, then at varying speeds. Parry 3 and riposte to the head.*

Half-Feint

4. *Use the same drill as #3. Your partner will be advancing and retreating. Maintain the distance and react against the attack with parry and riposte at the appropriate time.*
5. *From short distance, your partner attacks to the flank and then quickly retreats. From the half-feint position, take parry 3 and riposte with a lunge.*
6. *From middle distance, half-feint position: Your partner attacks with a long lunge to the flank and recovers to on-guard quickly. Make a short retreat from the attack, parry 3, and riposte to the partner's head with a lunge or flèche.*

All these drills can be used for learning ripostes to the head after parry 4. For learning the riposte from parry 5, there are specific drills.

Riposte to the Head After Parry 5

As your partner attacks toward your head, parry 5. Your partner leaves his or her blade in the cut position on the strong part of your blade. Execute the riposte in two sequences:

1. Pass your blade under your opponent's saber by moving the point backward and to the right. The saber's cutting edge is now directed forward and up.
2. Conclude the cut by using the wrist-finger action followed by an arm extension forward.

Having learned the proper sequence of these movements, practice uninterrupted ripostes from parry 5.

Avoid the following mistakes:

Taking the parry too soon, instead of against the final action of the attack.

Reaching for the opponent's blade instead of blocking and absorbing the cut. This leads to a wide amplitude in the parrying motion, which makes another parry impossible. It also slows the riposte because the fencer must overcome the inertia of the defensive motion. Only as the fencer reaches a higher level of technical proficiency should the beat-parry be introduced.

Failing to turn the cutting edge of the saber toward the opponent's blade for defense. As a result, the fencer may loose the grip or get hit with a whip-over.

Riposting with the retreat. This is usually caused by the fencer holding ground with the parry but retreating with the riposte.

Retreating too far with a parry, breaking the distance, and as a result being unable to riposte successfully.

Ripostes to the Flank or Chest

Ripostes to the flank or chest are best learned when the techniques of riposting to the head and attacking to the flank and chest are firmly established. The structure of the ripostes to the flank and chest is very similar to the simple attacks already described. There are, however, some points to remember:

In a *riposte from parry 4*, the guard moves toward the target and simultaneously to the right with the final position in the fencing plane (outside line).

The technique for the *chest cut from parry 5* looks like the riposte to the head, but the point (for a right-handed fencer) is carried to the right of the head, and the cutting edge is directed down-inward and should land on the opponent's upper chest or shoulder.

In the *riposte to the flank from parry 5*, the entire arm lowers the saber in order to avoid hitting the opponent's guard and then moves forward to deliver the riposte.

LEARNING EXPERIENCE—RIPOSTES TO THE FLANK OR CHEST

In the first stage of training, all drills for learning and perfecting the technique of parries and ripostes to the flank and chest are preplanned.

From short distance, half-feint hand position:

1.   *Partner attempts to cut to the flank, then recovers to a predetermined 5th position. Parry 3 and riposte to the flank, then slowly recover to on-guard.*
2.   *Partner attacks to the mask, then recovers to 5th position. Parry 5 and riposte to the flank, then slowly recover.*
3.   *Partner attacks to the chest, then recovers to 4th position. Parry 4 and riposte to the flank, then slowly recover.*

The same drills may be used to practice ripostes to the chest—for example, the partner always returns to 3rd position after an unsuccessful attack.

Ripostes to the Opening Target Area

Riposting to the opening target is the next step in improving a fencer's defense. The fencer uses a preplanned parry and needs to choose which target area to attack.

1. *From short distance, your partner attacks the same target (head, chest, or flank), then recovers to a non-predetermined position. After taking the preplanned parry, you find the opening target area and riposte.*
2. *From middle distance, your partner attacks to a predetermined target with a lunge, then recovers to a non-predetermined position. After taking the pre-planned parry, find the opening target area and riposte with a lunge.*

Note: After parrying, the fencer should pause briefly to determine the opening target area.

Determining the Line of Attack

The ability to determine the direction of an opponent's attack and to react in time with an appropriate parry is a vital skill for survival. Drills for acquiring these skills are in the accompanying Learning Experience.

All attacks must be executed at a slow, uninterrupted pace.

From middle distance:
1. *While you are in a half-feint hand position, your partner slowly attacks any of your targets with the lunge. Determine the line of attack, use an appropriate parry without retreat, then riposte to the head.*
2. *Repeat the drill in #1 with your partner making a longer lunge, causing you to retreat with a parry, then riposte.*
3. *Your partner attacks any target area, forcing you to use an appropriate parry, then recovers to 5th position. After making the parry, riposte to the flank.*
4. *Your partner leads, advancing and retreating, while you maintain the distance. Your partner attacks to any of the target areas by lunging or advancing. Determine the line of attack, make the appropriate parry, then riposte to the mask.*
5. *Now you lead, advancing and retreating. Your partner maintains the distance and chooses the moment to attack any target during his or her footwork. Use an appropriate parry, then riposte to the chest.*

The following drills closely simulate conditions in an actual bout.

From middle distance:
1. *While you are in half-feint hand position, your partner may attack with a lunge to any target area with maximum speed. Make the appropriate parry and riposte.*
2. *Your partner leads by advancing and retreating and attacks an open target at*

different moments during his or her footwork. Make the appropriate parry and riposte.

3. *Same as #2 above, reverse roles.*

From long distance:

4. *Lead by advancing and retreating smoothly. With each advance, turn the cutting edge forward as the leading leg advances. With each retreat, as the rear leg moves backward, move the saber back to 3rd position. While keeping distance, your partner attacks any target at different times:*
   a. *Against your advance*
   b. *During the pause between your steps*
   c. *At the beginning of your retreat*

The task is to determine the line of your partner's attack, to make the appropriate parry, and then riposte.

5. *The Riposte Game: This drill should be performed at first without footwork. It may then be developed—for example, with advances and retreats, lunges, advance-lunges, and balestras.*

   Start by attacking slowly into one of the three target areas. Your partner parries and slowly ripostes to an open target. Then it is your turn to choose the correct parry and execute slowly a counter-riposte. Continue the sequence.

Note: It is imperative to practice this drill at a slow tempo. The defender must not withdraw the arm prematurely. By determining the direction of an attack or riposte, the fencer makes the appropriate parry at the final moment and then ripostes to the open target.

By practicing attacks and parries slowly, fencers should develop a feeling for the proper execution of any fencing action. You will soon be able to accelerate your tempo and execute these movements with your partner in simulated competition using a variety of footwork.

HIGHLIGHTS

1. Define the terms *position* and *parry*.
2. Demonstrate extending the weapon arm for a point thrust from the 3rd position and returning to on-guard.
3. At short distance, demonstrate:
   a. Parry 5 and riposte to the head.
   b. Parry 3 and riposte to the chest.
   c. Parry 4 and riposte to the flank.
4. At middle distance, demonstrate riposte with a lunge, utilizing the combinations in number 3 above.

ADVANCED SKILLS

Attack with One Feint

When an opponent reveals a tendency to cover a target by attempting to parry against a simple attack, a fencer must be ready to use a feint attack.

The *feint* is the movement that only gives the *impression* that a real attack is being launched. It is designed to elicit a parry from one's opponent.

As the opponent attempts to parry, the attacking blade evades the parry and cuts (or thrusts) to an exposed target area. The feint toward the target accelerates in the same fashion as a real cut, but the arm is not completely extended at the end of the feint. The final action is achieved by changing the line of the attack with a cutting motion using the wrist and fingers, with limited participation of the forearm, coinciding with full arm extension.

The time to begin a feint depends on the distance between the opponents. The execution of a feint must start at the moment when the distance is favorable to create a believable threat to an opponent's target.

The principle of the single feint is that it must be deep enough and swift enough to give the impression that it is a genuine attack. Only then will the feint draw the opponent's reaction to parry.

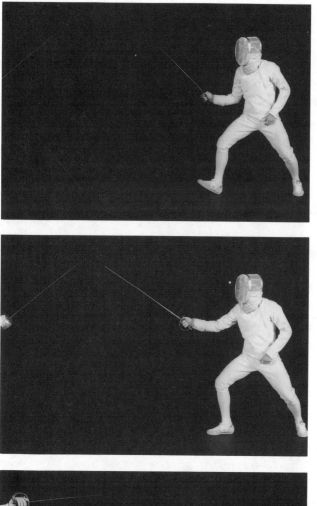

Attack with Feint

1

2

3

LEARNING EXPERIENCE—ATTACK WITH ONE FEINT

1. At short distance, both fencers in 3rd position:
    a. Feint at random to the head or flank with half-extension, pause, and recover to 3rd position after each feint.
    b. Slowly feint with half-extension to the head. Your partner reacts with parry 5 as your blade nears his or her head. Deceive the parry and cut to the flank. Both recover.
    c. Your partner is in 5th position. Execute a feint to the flank with half-extension. Your partner reacts with parry 3 as your blade nears its target. Deceive the parry and cut to the head. Both recover.
2. From middle distance (short lunge): The short-distance drills described above may be used for drills at middle distance. (Note: The final cut should be executed simultaneously with or before completion of the lunge.)
3. From long distance (a little beyond middle distance): With your rear foot completing the short advance, feint to the head with a half-extension of your arm. As your partner reacts with parry 5, deceive the parry and cut to the flank with a lunge.

As you become more familiar with this type of a feint attack, practice other attacks with feint: flank-head, flank-chest, chest-flank, head-chest, chest-head, head-point, point-head, flank-point, point-flank.

Once you have mastered the proper technique for cuts and feints, practice accelerating the attack smoothly. *Note:* The feint must be coordinated with the moment that you approach your opponent in sufficient distance to threaten your opponent effectively.

LEARNING EXPERIENCE—MORE FEINT-ATTACKS

4. From middle distance (lunge), your partner slowly changes positions from 3rd to 5th and back. When a target begins to open, execute a feint with half-extension. As your partner reacts, continue the attack with lunge to the opening target area.
5. From long distance, use drill #4 with an advance-lunge.
6. Your partner advances in 5th position and retreats in 3rd. While you hold your ground, choose the proper moment to attack:
    a. With the lunge into your opponent's advance, use a flank feint-head cut.
    b. With an advance-lunge, when your opponent retreats use a head feint—flank cut.
7. Using drill #6, maintain your distance and choose the correct moment to execute a feint-attack with either a lunge or an advance-lunge.

Defense Against Attack with One Feint

To defend against an attack with a feint, the fencer must practice (1) not reacting to the feint and (2) parrying only the actual cut. The fencer should remain relaxed against the feint. This is practiced starting from 3rd, 4th, or 5th position. The instructor or partner feints and cuts to each line.

But parrying just the final cut is not the only way to defend against a feint attack. If the defender does not react to a feint, a cunning attacker will make a direct cut. Therefore, in order to draw the attacker's cut, the defender can use "defensive second intention" by first showing a false half-parry (feint-parry) in reaction to the feint and parrying the final cut. However, it is absolutely essential to introduce these actions as entirely preplanned at this level of fencing education.

When learning to defend against a feint attack, it is important for the fencer to use small, restricted movements. In order to teach this, the instructor first stops the fencer after the half-parry (feint-parry or false-parry) position is established to check for corrections:

Is the shoulder relaxed?
Is the saber in proper position?
Were the movements small and restricted?

When satisfied with the fencer's position, the instructor attempts the final attack, which is parried by the fencer. The saber should move from the false parry to a real one in a smooth, relaxed manner without stiff, hard, jerky, or abrupt movements.

LEARNING EXPERIENCE—PARRYING THE ATTACK WITH ONE FEINT

1. *From short distance, your partner alternates making feints and direct cuts in the same line. Parry the real attacks at the last moment, and refrain from reacting to the feints.*
2. *From long distance, with the advance, your partner executes a feint and then attacks with lunge to any target. Hold your ground—do not react to the feint. Use appropriate parry against the final cut and riposte to the head. The fencer's primary attention is directed toward identifying the line of the real attack and the choice of an appropriate parry.*

After succeeding with the previous exercise, as the speed and length of your opponent's attack increase, use a small retreat with your real parry.

The Compound Parry

The execution of more than one parrying movement against the same attack is a compound parry. Having learned compound parries while in a stationary position, the fencer should practice them with retreat. In so doing, the fencer is given *distance* in addition to *time* to execute a compound parry.

The feint parry is made with the step taken by the rear foot; the second, real, parry is taken with the completion of the retreat—that is, with the recovery of the leading foot. The fencer completes the retreat in a perfect on-guard position and executes a riposte.

At first, the action is practiced slowly. The movement may even be dissected and each part learned separately. The component parts can then be joined together to form a smooth, fast flowing action.

LEARNING EXPERIENCE—MORE DEFENSE AGAINST THE FEINT ATTACK

3. *Your partner feints to the chest with his or her advance. While holding your ground, react to the feint with half-parry 4. When your partner concludes the attack with a lunge to the flank, parry 3 with a short retreat, riposte to the head.*

This drill should be practiced against any single feint attacks.
Note: For learning purposes, all attacks and parries are executed slowly and smoothly.

Avoid the following mistakes:

Reacting too broadly to the feint with the parry, causing delay in movement to the final parry.
Improper coordination between hand and foot work.
Leaning back instead of retreating.
Reacting to the feint too soon, allowing the opponent to develop his or her attack with multiple feints.

Counteroffense

Attack on the Preparation

Once a solid defensive technique and proper defensive reactions are developed, it is time to learn the counteroffensive actions.

Most beginners, when caught by surprise, naturally react to an opponent's attack with a counterattack, rather than parrying, but because the counterattack does not give right-of-way to the fencer attacked, another skill must be learned. Success with parrying develops confidence against any kind of attack. Developing confidence in a defensive system based on parrying is made easier because beginning fencers know and use only a limited number of attacks.

After mastering the simple attacks and facing opponents with a stronger defense, a fencer—following the logic of survival—should develop a wide variety of compound attacks to overcome the opponent's defense. That would lead, in turn, to discovering ways to oppose the compound attack. Besides the parry and riposte, these are counteroffensive actions, such as the attack on the preparation, the counterattack (stop-cut, stop-thrust), and the point-in-line. These are all used as remedies against compound and prolonged attacks, opponents who hesitate with the final action of an attack, opponents who expose a target before the final cut, and so on.

LEARNING EXPERIENCE—ATTACK ON THE PREPARATION

1. *From middle distance, your partner leads, and you maintain distance. The partner alternates between an attack to your head or just an advance, holding his or her arm in the on-guard position.*
    a. *Parry 5 and riposte against the attack. Do not react against the advance—stay in place.*
    b. *Retreat against the attack. Attack to the head against the advance.*
    c. *Parry 5 and riposte against the attack. Attack against the advance.*

Note: *The actions in this Learning Experience are directing you to attack on your opponent's preparations or to counterattack.*

2. *From long distance, your partner attacks with an advance and lunges to your chest.*
    a. *Hold your ground against the advance. Use parry 4 and riposte against the attack. If the opponent's lunge is long, use a short retreat.*
    b. *Attack to the head using a lunge or flèche against the careless advance.*

The Stop-Cut

An effective stop-cut is a vital element in the defensive game.

The instructor should preferably introduce *stop-cuts* to the hand or wrist in the individual lesson. The stop-cut is taught by cutting on the outside, top, inside, or bottom of the wrist with either the cutting edge or the back edge of the blade. Start with the stop-cut to the top of the wrist.

It takes a great deal of blade and distance control, as well as a sense of timing, to execute a proper stop-cut. The hand and forearm, which are minimal targets, usually move and can easily be protected. Even when the stop-cut is properly executed, success is not always guaranteed because the opponent's blade still has a chance to

Stop-Cut to the
Underneath Area

Stop-Cut to the
Outside Area

reach the target in tempo. Therefore, it is advisable to make a stop-cut with a retreat, which usually should be followed by parry and riposte.

The stop-cut is executed by reaching out with the cut to the opponent's hand while at the same time pulling back with the rear foot. The parry is executed with the landing of the leading foot. The fencer should now be in a well-balanced position and at the perfect distance for a riposte.

A well-rounded structure in defense is essential for success, but do not rush into this or you may lose the proper parrying instincts. The stop-cut takes advantage of any incorrectly executed attack because the stop-cut, striking the nearer target (hand or forearm) will arrive sooner than the opponent's attack to any further target. This will make the opponent leery of attacking for fear of being hit.

The stop-cut must arrive a tempo ahead of the final movement of the attack to gain right-of-way.

LEARNING EXPERIENCE—THE STOP-CUT

1. *From middle distance, your partner advances and retreats. Maintain the distance. At various times, your partner prolongs the advance and extends his or her arm. Make a stop-cut to the outside of your partner's hand and step back.*
2. *Your partner alternates between a short, fast attack to the flank, and long feint to the flank while advancing. Your reaction should be:*
    a.   *To parry 3 and riposte on the fast attack (holding your ground)*
    b.   *Stop-cut the outside of your partner's wrist on the long feint with a retreat*
3. *Your partner attempts to attack the head with slow advance. While retreating, make a stop-cut to the inside of the hand, then parry 5 and riposte to the chest. (With the rear foot in motion, make a stop-cut; as the leading foot moves, execute a parry; holding your ground, riposte.)*
4. *Your partner attempts to attack the flank while slowly advancing. While retreating, you cut the outside of his or her hand, then parry 3 and riposte.*

5. *Your partner attempts to attack the chest while slowly advancing. While retreating, you cut top of the hand, then parry 4 and riposte.*

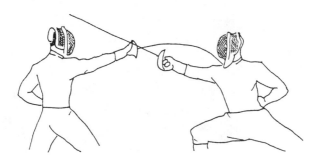

Thrust with Opposition

Thrust with Opposition

Point-in-Line

An aggressive fencer may be deterred from attacking, or may be required to spend more time preparing the attack, when the defender makes use of a *point-in-line*, where the arm is straight and the point is threatening the opponent's target. This approach may gain the defender the time and opportunity to employ a tactic from his or her own pool of resources.

Note: The defender should establish point-in-line before the actual attack has started, or it becomes a counterattack with the point (a stop-thrust).

The Counter-Time

The counter-time is an offensive action of second intention to lure the opponent into an anticipating counterattacking reaction and utilizing it accordingly. By insinuating a compound attack or attempting to take the opponent's blade, the fencer convinces the opponent that one can score with the stop-cut. Having lured his or her adversary into a counterattack, the fencer parries while approaching the opponent and scores in second intention.

LEARNING EXPERIENCE—COUNTER-TIME

1. *From short distance, as you make a half-feint to the head, your partner attempts to score a stop-cut to the outside of your hand. You react with parry 3 and riposte to the head.*
2. *From middle distance, do the same as above, with half-advance. After parrying, execute a riposte to the head with a lunge.*
3. *From long distance, as you attempt to engage your opponent's weapon into outside high line (3rd) with an advance, he or she deceives it with a disengage and threatens with the point. Parry 4 and riposte with a lunge to the head.*
4. *Execute a false attack with a short balestra, inviting the opponent to attempt a stop-cut under your hand while retreating. As your opponent does this, withdraw your hand, permitting the stop-cut to fall short. Finish the attack with a flèche aiming at the chest.*

HIGHLIGHTS

1. From middle distance, demonstrate the proper way to execute beat-4–head cut with the cutting edge of your saber.
2. From long distance, demonstrate the same attack as #1 with half-advance and flèche.
3. State the purpose of the feint and the main feature to consider in its execution.
4. From middle distance, demonstrate a lunge with a flank feint-point thrust attack.
5. From long distance, demonstrate a half-advance flèche with a point feint–flank cut attack.
6. From middle distance, demonstrate a lunge with a chest feint–flank cut attack.
7. From middle distance, demonstrate a lunge with a head feint–chest cut attack.
8. Describe the defender's "half-parry" to a feint.
9. Describe and demonstrate how a defender employs a "defensive of second intention" action to a feint attack.
10. What is meant by a compound parry?
11. What does a defender gain when he or she retreats before parrying?
12. Demonstrate how to defend against a flank feint–chest cut attack from long distance.

13. With a partner, demonstrate the proper timing for executing a successful stop-cut, to the outside of the forearm, against attack with the feint to the head from long distance.
14. Why are most stop-cuts executed to the opponent's hand or forearm?
15. Why is it advisable to execute a stop-cut with a retreat?
16. Describe and demonstrate when and how to execute a counterattack to the opponent's head with a flèche.
17. Describe and define "point in line."
18. List three ways in which a point-thrust may be used.
19. Demonstrate the proper execution of a point-thrust from engagement in 3rd position.
20. Demonstrate the recovery to on-guard (3rd) from the "point-in-line" position.
21. Describe "counter-time."
22. Demonstrate two examples of counter-time.

4

Épée

INTRODUCTION

This chapter offers a practical approach to the instruction of épée fencing in the United States. Accordingly, many principles and ideas are borrowed from schools of épée around the world. It is hoped that an American school of épée will emerge from this melting pot of theories and techniques.

This chapter is dedicated to my fencing masters: Marisa Cerani, Marcello Lodetti, Janos Kevey, Arturo Volpini, and Istvan Danosi. —Gil Pezza.

THE DEVELOPMENT OF ÉPÉE FENCING

In more recent times, modern competitive épée fencing gained impetus and popularity following the organization of the Olympic Games held in Athens, Greece, in 1896. After the suppression of duelling in France and England, and later in Germany and Italy, with the modification of the duelling sword, épée fencing developed into a sporting event. Over the years, three schools of épée developed: the classical school (c. 1900), the East European school (c. 1959), and the German school of Tauberbischofsheim (at Tauberg, c. 1973).

The Classical School

The popularity of competitive épée fencing can be traced to the Olympic Games of Paris in 1900, which included épée events for professionals and amateurs and one combined event for both. Thereafter, until 1959, team gold medals at the Olympic Games and World Championships were won by Italy (15), France (10), and Belgium (2).

In this period, the French classical school influenced all other European schools. Maître Baudry, founder of the French school of épée, and his followers Sulzbacher, Renauld, and Bruneau de Labori, were instrumental in spreading the seeds of épée throughout Europe. In Italy these seeds were cultivated by Maestro Giuseppe Mangiarotti, who founded the Northern Italian school of épée in Milan.

The East European School

In 1959 the Hungarian épée team won its first gold medal at the World Championships in Budapest. This was the first time an Eastern European nation had captured the gold medal in the épée team event. The years between 1959 and 1973 witnessed the emergence of Hungarian, Soviet, and Polish schools of épée. These schools emphasized tactics over technique.

In this period, team gold medals were distributed to Hungary (6), Soviet Union (3), France (3), Poland (1), and Italy (1). No doubt the success of the East European teams was in no small way attributable to government subsidy and organizational support.

The German School at Tauberg

The German épée team captured its first gold medal at the World Championships in Göteborg, Sweden, in 1973. The German school of Tauberg was founded by Meister E. Beck, whose method of teaching simplified the technical game of épée while maximizing the powerful "offense" capabilities of the modern athlete-fencer. Meister Beck introduced a method of training in which fencers were channeled through successive stages of apprenticeship with specialized fencing masters. In this respect, the German school of Tauberg may be considered the first modern "factory" of fencers.

From 1973 to 1990, team gold medals were awarded to West Germany (5), Sweden (4), France (4), USSR (3), Italy (2), and Hungary (2). Included in these figures are the first two Women's Épée World Championships in 1989 and 1990.

LEARNING EXPERIENCE—ÉPÉE HISTORY

Interview fencing masters trained in European fencing schools. Interview fencing masters trained in America. Compare the teaching techniques demonstrated by their students in competition.

THE WEAPON AND EQUIPMENT FOR ÉPÉE FENCING

Ever since the seventeenth century, the foil has been the basic training weapon in preparation for use of the duelling sword. Over the years, the foil fencing target became restricted to include only the torso, whereas the target for the duelling sword encompassed the entire body.

An inevitable conflict of philosophy regarding the preferred sequence of training arose among fencing masters. Those who believed it was imperative for the fencer to learn to use the foil before starting épée training were in disagreement with those who considered it more expeditious to start the student immediately with the fundamentals using the épée.

In most recent times, there has been a move to encourage younger fencers to participate in the sport. A smaller, lighter version of the regulation épée has been developed, allowing them to practice épée rather than foil. The author believes that this is not a significant issue in the development of the fencer. For safety reasons, it is best to group the young épée fencers according to body height and weight. Bouting or sparring outside one's height and weight category should be allowed only under supervision.

The Épée

The épée has five parts—the point, the blade, the bell guard, the handle, and the pommel. The total length of the weapon should be limited to 110 centimeters, with the total weight not to exceed 770 grams.

The Point (Button/Tip)

The electrical point is cylindrical in shape. The diameter of the barrel is at least 7.7 millimeters, and the diameter of the electrical tip (crown) is 8.0 millimeters.

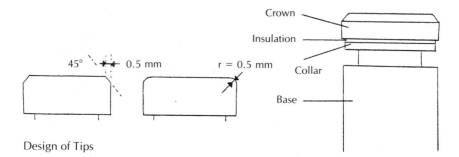

Design of Tips

For a touch to be registered by the scoring apparatus, pressure of more than 750 grams must be exerted on the tip. Before the start of a bout, the official must test the épée with a 750-gram weight to be sure the weapon meets the specifications shown above. The official must use a 1.5-millimeter gauge to test the stroke of the point, to be sure the point will travel at least 1.5 millimeters before registering on the scoring apparatus. A gauge is then used to determine that the point will travel at least 0.5 millimeters before registering.

The button of the point for nonelectrical épée must also conform to the specifications required for electrical épées.

The Blade

The blade, which must be made of steel, is fashioned in a triangular shape without cutting edges and mounted with the groove uppermost. The blade should be straight, and any curve to the blade must be less than 1 centimeter in a vertical plane. The exposed blade must not exceed 90 centimeters. To ensure safety and equity for all contestants, it is illegal to alter a blade by grinding or filing.

LEARNING EXPERIENCE—THE BLADE AND POINT

1. Examine electrical and nonelectrical blades. What are the fundamental differences? What are the differences in the points?
2. How much variation is allowed in the bend of the blade?

The Bell Guard

The bell guard protects the fencer's hand. It must be circular in shape, 13.5 centimeters in diameter, and between 3.0 and 5.5 centimeters deep.

The Handle

The two types of handles used in present-day épée fencing are the French (straight) handle and the pistol (orthopedic) handle. Which to use may be determined by one's individual physical hand characteristics—for example, a person with long, flexible fingers will adapt more easily to the French handle, while fencers with short fingers and broad hands may prefer the pistol handle.

The handle is mounted on the tang of the blade.

The Pommel

The parts of the French épée are held together by means of the pommel (locknut) at the exposed end of the tang. Conversely, the locknut for the pistol grip is inserted into the handle.

LEARNING EXPERIENCE—BELL GUARD, HANDLE, AND POMMEL

1. *Assemble an épée with a French handle.*
2. *Assemble an épée with a pistol handle.*

The Body Cord

The body cord is a required part of equipment for electrical fencing. It is worn inside the sleeve of the weapon arm of the fencing jacket and protrudes through the opening in the palm of the fencing glove to be attached to the plug inside the guard. The opposite end is attached by a three-prong male plug to a reel at the rear end of the strip. The body cord must be in working order at all times. If it fails to function, a replacement must be immediately available at the competition strip. The maximum electrical resistance for the body cord is 1 ohm.

HIGHLIGHTS

1. Identify the parts of an electrical épée.
2. Identify the two basic handle shapes.
3. State how all parts of the épée are locked in place.
4. Describe the tip of an electrical épée blade and how it functions.
5. Describe how the body cord is attached for competition.

BASIC CONCEPTS OF AN ÉPÉE BOUT

Method for Scoring a Touch

The épée is a thrusting weapon. Therefore, scoring is accomplished only with the point. The épée, the counterpart of the duelling sword, has no rules governing right-of-way, as do foil and saber. Therefore, regardless of who initiates the action, the épée fencer who scores first is awarded the touch. In épée the double-touch is common, with a point awarded to each fencer.

Judging Touches in Épée

Épée competitions are judged using an electrical scoring machine calibrated to register a double-touch if the difference of time between the two touches is less than 1/20th to 1/25th of a second. The time frame of 1/25th of a second is a fundamental factor in épée fencing. All tactical and technical considerations are derived from this time frame.

Materiality of the Touch

Only hits indicated by the electrical machine can be taken into consideration for judging the materiality of touches. Touches may be annulled by the referee (until just recently called the president or director) if action was started before the command "Fence" or after "Halt," if the points of the épées meet, or if the touch was made on any object other than the opponent, such as on the ground outside the metallic strip.

Furthermore, the referee must annul the last score made if the touch scored was made on the opponent's bell guard, if the touch properly made does not cause the machine to register the hit, or if the machine registers a touch caused by any movement by either or both fencers without touching the target. If a double-touch is registered by an established score and a doubtful touch (due to failure of the electrical machine or by uncertainty of the referee), the fencer who scored the certain touch may choose to accept the double-touch or ask to have it annulled.

Duration of the Bout

In épée, bouts are normally for five touches, with a time limit of four minutes per bout. If because of a double-touch both fencers score the maximum number of touches, they must continue the bout for one or more supplementary touches until time expires. Before each bout, the referee will determine by lot and announce which fencer will be the winner of the bout if time runs out with the score tied. There are no longer double defeats in épée. In direct-elimination bouts, the referee will announce *before* each bout which fencer had the higher seed into the initial table. That fencer will be the winner of the bout if time runs out with the score tied. If there is a tie in the seeding into the table, the referee will determine by lot and announce before the bout starts which fencer will be the winner of the bout if time runs out with the score tied.

A direct-elimination bout is divided into three rounds of three minutes duration each with a one-minute break between rounds. In other words, direct-elimination bouts are for fifteen touches. When the fifteenth touch is awarded, regardless of time, the bout is over.

On the other hand, if the allotted time has expired, the fencer who has scored more touches than his or her opponent is the victor. However, the number of touches required for the bout must be added to total the maximum. For example, if the score was 3 to 2, each fencer would receive 2 touches to bring the final score to 5 to 4.

LEARNING EXPERIENCE—BASIC BOUT RULES

1. How does one score a touch with the épée?
2. How are épée competitions judged?
3. What is meant by "materiality of the touch"?
4. What is the duration of time for a five-touch bout?
5. If the score is tied and time has elapsed, what is the outcome?
6. In a direct elimination bout, is it possible for both fencers to be listed as losers?
7. If time has expired in a bout in which Fencer A has four touches and B has one touch, what is the final score?

The Target

In épée fencing, touches may be scored to any part of the body. The target in épée traditionally comprises two groups:

The *advanced target*, which includes the weapon arm, the leading leg and foot, and, in the lunge position, the mask.

The *central target*, which includes the torso, the mask in the on-guard position, and in short distance (close quarters) the trailing leg and the trailing arm.

In modern fencing, however, the advanced target is best described as *the closest target to the point of the épée, at any given time during the fencing bout*. This definition suits the modern épée fencer, who must recognize the best target area available at any given moment.

Épée Target (entire body)

BASIC SKILLS

The Épée Positions

On-Guard

The on-guard position is the position from which the fencer is balanced and ready to attack, defend, or counterattack. Because the target area in épée includes the entire body, *the on-guard position in épée should have the feet separated about one and a half fencer's foot-lengths apart.* This position provides better balance and helps protect the advanced target areas. The knees should be flexed, allowing quick and effective mobility. The formerly accepted classical épée on-guard position—with weapon fully extended—is no longer generally prescribed.

On-Guard

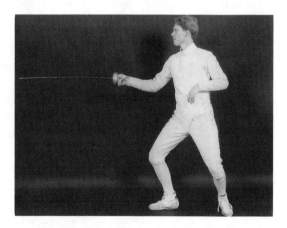

The *weapon-arm* should be relaxed at the elbow, with the point of the épée straight ahead and slightly downward, directed toward the opponent's guard. The *body* should be held erect with the weight on the leading leg. The fencer should *stand on the ball of the trailing foot,* which should be slightly angled toward the leading foot, thus allowing the fencer to move quickly and to change direction effectively. The *leading foot* should remain pointed directly forward. The *trailing arm* should be relaxed at the shoulder and kept low. The *shoulders* should be angled slightly forward toward the opponent to maximize the fencer's speed on the strip.

The Grip

The épée utilizing the French handle is held with the groove of the blade facing upward. The thumb should be on the top of the handle, the tip of the thumb about an inch away from the guard. The lower part of the handle should lie on the middle phalange of the index finger. The remaining three fingers should close around the handle. If opponents use strong attacks against the blade, one can move the thumb closer to the guard for better control and manipulation of the weapon. The pistol grip is formed to fit the natural position of the fencer's hand when holding the weapon. With either handle, the thumb and the index finger guide and control the point.

Lines and Positions

Because the closest advanced target is generally the wrist and forearm, the épée fencer must protect that target area at all times. For maximum protection, it is necessary to understand the meaning of fencing lines—namely, the inside line (representing the chest side), the outside line (representing the back side), the high line (representing area above the guard position), and the low line (representing area below the guard position).

To protect the wrist and forearm, the weapon hand should be held toward supination (palm up) rather than toward pronation (palm down).

6th Position

In 6th position, the weapon hand is toward supination, the forearm is level with the elbow, and the arm is slightly extended. The bell guard is somewhat turned toward

6th Position

the outside line, protecting the wrist, the forearm, and the backside of the body. The point of the blade is directed slightly downward at the opponent's target (the biceps).

8th Position

In 8th position, the weapon hand is toward supination, the forearm is horizontal, and the elbow is partially flexed, with the point of the blade lower than the hand. The blade and the guard protect the lower outside line.

8th Position

2nd Position

2nd Position

In 2nd position, the weapon hand is in pronation, the forearm is horizontal, and the elbow is slightly flexed, with the point of the blade lower than the hand. The blade and guard position is similar to 8th position. The 2nd position is particularly effective during infighting.

1st, 3rd, 4th, and 7th Positions

Descriptions of 1st, 3rd, 4th, and 7th positions are in Chapter 2 of this book, on Foil Fencing. If used judiciously and with opposition (using closed lines while maintaining control of opponent's weapon), any of these four positions may become an effective action.

4th Position

Footwork

The Lunge and Recovery

The quality of a lunge—athletic velocity, timing, and judgment of distance—is determined by the fencer's training and physical attributes.

Executing the lunge may be accomplished by moving forward toward the opponent. This is performed by pushing off from the ball of the trailing foot as the leading leg is thrust forward in a pendular motion, the heel skimming the floor without elevating the knee. As the lunge is completed, the leading lower leg should be in a vertical position above the center of the foot, the trailing leg extended, the trailing foot kept firmly on the floor, and the trailing arm extended parallel to the trailing leg. The length of the lunge is determined by the intended target.

To recover from the lunge, flex the trailing knee, push backward with the heel of the leading foot and pull backward by actively bending the trailing leg, and return the leading leg and trailing arm to original on-guard position, weapon-arm extended.

To recover toward the opponent, flex the trailing leg as body weight shifts slightly forward, and bring the trailing leg forward the necessary distance toward the leading foot. In every action of the lunge and recovery, the trunk of the body should remain erect, staying as far as possible away from the opponent's weapon point.

Thrust with Lunge

The backward lunge is unique to épée. It is executed when there is a forward movement by the opponent and is performed by extending the trailing leg backward while pushing off with the leading foot. This manner of lunging allows the fencer to maintain an offensive stance while retreating.

Because épée fencing has no rule of right-of-way, the fencer can utilize every permissible technique to score. Consequently, because a fencer is most vulnerable during recovery from the lunge, he or she should exercise the following options:

Recover as quickly as possible.
Remain in the lunge.
Attack with a flèche.

The correct choice will depend on:

The physical characteristics of the fencer.
The athletic ability (speed, agility, endurance) of each fencer.
The distance between the two fencers.
The reaction of the opponent.
The position of the blade of the fencer in relation to that of the opponent on completion of the lunge.

The Lunge

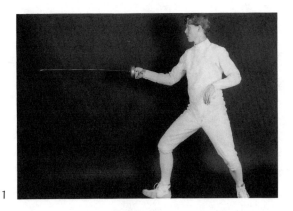

1

2

3

LEARNING EXPERIENCE—THE LUNGE AND RECOVERY

1. *Practice executing the lunge with the toes of the leading foot lifted off the floor. Lunging 10 minutes a day will help a fencer learn to maintain balance.*
2. *Practice executing the recovery to the on-guard position from the lunge. Practice recovering 10 minutes a day, keeping the leading foot one inch off the ground for 2 seconds.*
3. *Practice executing the recovery forward to on-guard position 10 minutes a day.*

The Advance and Retreat

The *advance,* or step forward, must be short to reduce the chances of being hit on your offensive preparation.

The advance can be executed in two ways:

1. By moving the leading foot first between 1 and $1\frac{1}{2}$ foot lengths, then moving the trailing foot an equal distance.
2. By moving the trailing foot first, then the leading foot in similar fashion, as in 1.

In both instances, be ready to attack if the opportunity presents itself. The body weight should be on the leading leg.

The *retreat* also may be executed in two ways, varying the length of the step:

1. By moving the trailing leg first, then moving the leading leg an equal distance, assuming the on-guard position.
2. By moving the leading leg first, then the trailing leg. (This technique gives the fencer the opportunity to remove the advanced target area more speedily from the opponent's threatening point.)

LEARNING EXPERIENCE—THE ADVANCE AND RETREAT

1. *Practice advancing and retreating rhythmically.*
2. *Practice advancing and retreating using varying rhythms.*
3. *Practice the alternate technique of advancing and retreating, varying the length of each step.*

The Jump Forward and the Balestra

The *jump forward* serves two functions: (1) It draws the opponent's attack and/or counterattack and (2) it serves as a *preparation for attack*—that is, before lunging (balestra) or flèching.

The *balestra* used to be considered a dangerous move for the épée fencer because it gives the opponent an opportunity to score quickly with a counterattack. Recently, however, many world-class épée fencers have included this technique in their repertoires. The execution of the balestra is described in Chapters 2 and 3, on foil and saber.

Instructor (I) and Fencer (F). F is within middle distance from I's forearm.

1. F executes a short jump forward and makes an invitation by dropping the blade into 8th position. I thrusts to the top of F's wrist or forearm. F parries 6 and ripostes to the crook of I's arm and I's shoulder and mask.
2. F starts with the blade in 8th position. While executing a short jump forward, F raises the weapon to 6th position. I attempts to thrust to F's knee. F counterattacks to I's forearm, following with a quick parry 2—riposte to I's forearm, and remise to I's knee.
3. I exposes the wrist by dropping the blade into 8th position. F hits I's wrist with a short jump forward, followed by a quick lunge to I's knee using opposition in 8th.
4. F executes a short jump forward, presenting the blade. I attempts to engage the blade in 4th. F hits I on the wrist with a disengage. I presents the blade in F's outside line. F covers outside line with opposition 6 and lunges with a glide into I's chest.

Small Jumps (Bounces)

Small jumps, or bounces, are a footwork technique peculiar to épée fencing. When at close range, many épée fencers use small jumps while patiently waiting for an opportunity to strike. By executing small jumps in place, the fencer maintains the rhythmic flow of movement without having to advance or retreat significantly.

Tactically, a fencer may execute small jumps either *in place, during a retreat, or to move back and forth,* followed by a lunge or flèche attack; a counterattack, including a stop-thrust with blade angulation; or a defensive action.

This jumping technique needs to be used with caution. It may create a problem for a fencer who establishes a set rhythmic pattern and hence provide the opponent with an opportunity to attack. To avoid this, alternate the small jumps with advances and retreats, and vary both the speed and the amount of ground covered. By creating a nonrhythmic pattern, the fencer might disorient the opponent.

---

1. To develop rhythmic skill and endurance, practice skipping rope 10 minutes every day.

2. *From an erect position, execute small jumps on the balls of the feet, rising no more than one inch off the floor.*
3. *As in #2 above, land in an on-guard position.*
4. *From the on-guard position, execute small jumps on the balls of the feet, moving backward.*
5. *From the on-guard position, execute small jumps followed by a lunge or flèche.*
6. *From the on-guard position, execute small jumps, break the rhythm, then advance.*
7. *From the on-guard position, execute small jumps moving backward, then advance and jump back, then lunge or flèche.*

The Flèche

For a detailed description of the flèche, see Chapters 2 and 3, on foil and saber.

One should avoid executing the flèche when beyond middle (lunging) distance. It is also recommended that the fencer hit twice when executing the flèche—the first touch on the flèche, and the second immediately thereafter, while passing the opponent.

The flèche should be used with discretion. A fencer is most vulnerable upon completion of the flèche.

Flèche

Fencing Rules for the Flèche

The fencing rules for the flèche are quite specific. A touch made during the movement in which a fencer is attempting to *pass* the opponent is considered valid, but a touch made *after passing* is annulled. The opponent having parried or avoided being hit by the flèche attack may score a valid touch even by turning around. A fencer who by executing a flèche attack causes body contact without brutality or violence does not transgress the basic convention of épée fencing and thus commits no fault. On the other hand, a fencer who ends a flèche attack by jostling the opponent should be penalized. In addition, any score by the fencer at fault must be annulled.* (See the USFA Penalty Chart reproduced in Chapter 6.)

LEARNING EXPERIENCE—THE FLÈCHE

The instructor (I) should have the fencer (F) execute the flèche on the instructor's advance or preparation. I leads, engaging F's blade in 6th position. F is at middle distance from I's chest.

1. *I, while advancing, opens 6th line by releasing F's blade. F executes a flèche to I's chest, followed by a remise.*
2. *I, while advancing, raises the point of the épée about 2 inches. F executes a flèche with a glide in the 6th line to I's chest, followed by a remise.*
3. *I, while advancing, applies a small pressure in 6th against F's blade. F executes sudden counterpressure also in 6th (if both are right-handed or left-handed) with flèche to I's chest, followed by a remise.*
4. *I, while advancing, attempts a change of engagement. F avoids the change of engagement by using a disengage, flèches to I's chest, followed by a remise.*
5. *I, while advancing, beats F's blade in 6th and executes a short thrust to F's forearm. F parries 6 and ripostes with a flèche to I's chest, followed by a remise.*

Flèching from the Lunge

Flèching from the lunge can be executed in three ways. The choice will depend on the natural preference of the fencer and the blade action to be executed:

1. From the lunge, bring back the leading foot (2–4 inches), then execute the flèche. This method is useful when the fencer is executing a parry-riposte or an attack of second intention.
2. Execute the flèche as an extension of the lunge. As soon as the leading foot hits the ground, the leading leg becomes the instrument for the propelling force necessary for the flèche. This technique is useful against an opponent who holds the parry or who is slow with the riposte. The remise can then be employed following the flèche.
3. Execute the flèche as a redoublement from the lunge by bringing the trailing foot slightly forward. The redoublement is a second attack immediately after recovering either forward or backward from the lunge. Épée fencers employ the redoublement with a forward recovery especially to pursue an opponent who tends to retreat. (For further description of the redoublement, see Chapter 2 on Foil Fencing.)

---

*From "Fencing Rules," 1990 edition, published by the United States Fencing Association.

The Offense

Single Offensive Actions

For a detailed description of the straight thrust, the direct attack, the disengage, and the cutover (or flick), all of which can be utilized in épée fencing, see Chapter 2, Foil Fencing. Simple offensive maneuvers that are unique to épée are attacks to the knee, the foot, the wrist, the forearm, and the mask.

Foot Thrust

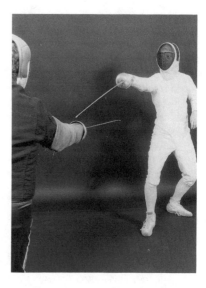

Hand Thrust

Compound Actions

Compound offensive maneuvers involve one or more feints before the final action arrives. Examples of compound attacks are:

The straight feint, disengage to score.
The disengage feint, a second disengage to score (one-two).
The one-two feint, a third disengage to score.
The feint low (under opponent's guard), hit high on biceps.

The final action can be directed toward the forearm, upper arm, knee, foot, head, torso, or mask.

For more details on compound actions, see Chapter 2.

Actions on the Blade

The purpose of actions on the blade, or "taking the blade," is to control the opponent's weapon until the final target is reached. Actions on the blade require preparation and determining just when to execute the attack. Examples of actions on the blade are opposition, transfer (bind), croisé, envelopment (circular transfer), and glide. These can be used either offensively or defensively.

Opposition is executed in all lines with the fencer controlling the opponent's blade in one line without releasing it until the action is completed. Blade control is attained by using the strong part of the épée against weaker section of opponent's blade.

Bind or *transfer* is an action carrying the opponent's blade from the high line to the diagonal low line—that is, 4th to 8th, or 6th to 7th. This may be also executed from the low line to the high line. Caution is necessary because the hand is open to counteraction if the fencer fails to control the opponent's blade.

Croisé is similar to the bind except that it terminates on the same side from which it originated—that is, 4th to 7th, 6th to 8th, and vice versa.

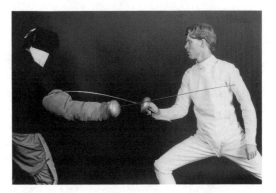

Thrust with Opposition 4

Envelopment (circular transfer) is a circular motion taking the opponent's blade in one line, without releasing it, and returning it to the same line. While executing the envelopment, the point progresses forward to the target.

The *glide* can best be described as continuous extension of the fencer's blade against the opponent's weapon, gliding along opponent's blade toward open target. To control the leverage, it is best to use the forté (strong) part of the blade against the foible (weak) part of opponent's blade. The glide is executed by taking the opponent's blade in one line and controlling it until completion of the action.

Thrust with Opposition 6   Thrust with Opposition 6 with Lunge

LEARNING EXPERIENCE—ACTIONS ON THE BLADE

1. *List four attacks with actions on the blade.*
2. *Which action requires a complete circular motion when taking the blade?*
3. *Which action requires a move from high line to low line when taking the blade?*

Secondary or Renewed Attacks

The remise, the reprise, and the redoublement are used as secondary attacks. The *remise* is the replacing of the point immediately after the original attack has failed. The *reprise* is normally executed as a replacement with a disengage while in lunge immediately following an unsuccessful attack. The *redoublement* is a second attack immediately following recovery from an unsuccessful attack.

For more detailed descriptions of these attacks, see Chapter 2 of this book, on foil fencing.

LEARNING EXPERIENCE—SECONDARY ATTACKS

1. *List three attacks that a fencer may employ when the initial attack fails.*
2. *Describe the differences between these three attacks.*

ADVANCED SKILLS—BLADEWORK

The Straight Thrust

The straight thrust originates from the elbow. In the early stages of learning the straight thrust, one should avoid strain caused by locking the deltoid (shoulder) muscle. To help relax the shoulder muscle, place the point as close to the target as possible, with minimal extension of the weapon arm.

Straight Thrust to the Forearm

LEARNING EXPERIENCE—STRAIGHT THRUST

With fencers in pairs:
Two fencers, A and B; A, with mask on, holds rolled-up glove in weapon hand; B without mask, holding épée. A and B stand at short distance, enabling B with a slight forward movement to hit the glove in A's hand.

1. *A raises hand exposing glove target; B hits target three times slowly.*
2. *As in #1 above, A changes the position of the target slightly between the first and second thrust, and between the second and third thrust.*
3. *As in #2 above, A moves the target slightly backward, forcing B to increase the reach of the thrust between touches.*
4. *As in #1 above, A moves back and forth; A stops before presenting target. B repeats actions as in #3 above.*
5. *A and B reverse roles and repeat exercises above.*

Drills for Straight Thrust

The following drills are for instructor (I) and fencer (F). F is at short distance from I's arm (the point of F's épée is a few inches away from the target).

1. *I leads, engaging F's blade in 6th position; I opens line; F hits crook of I's arm twice.*
2. *As in #1 above, but F hits I on the upper arm and chest.*

The Straight Thrust with Lunge

The lunge, an extension of the thrust, requires the fencer to synchronize these skills in order to thrust and lunge in proper sequence. This can be done by practicing alone, working in pairs, and practicing with an instructor.

Drills for Straight Thrust with Lunge

The following drill is for two fencers, A and B. Fencer A, wearing mask, holds rolled-up glove in weapon hand. B, with épée, wears no mask. A and B are at short distance. B using a slight forward movement of the forearm hits glove in A's hand. The glove may be moved up or down, to the right or left, at varying distances.

1. *A, holding glove out of sight, presents it in view at chest level. B hits glove twice.*
2. *A raises target. B initiates thrust toward glove as A retreats. B follows through with a lunge and hits target.*

The following drills are for instructor (I) and fencer (F):
At short distance, I leads by engaging F's blade in 6th position.

1. *I opens line. F hits crook of I's arm. I retreats. F lunges to I's upper arm.*
2. *I opens line. F begins thrust to crook of I's arm as I retreats. F follows with lunge to I's arm.*

Point Control

In épée, since the entire body is valid target, the fencer must learn point control in order to hit with the utmost precision. This skill must be emphasized early in the fencer's development. At the learning stages, it is most important for the fencer to execute the moves slowly and correctly until the fencer is consistently successful in hitting the target. Speed of execution will come with training and experience.

Drills for Point Control

The following drills are for two fencers, A and B. For lesson drills with the instructor, use the same drills, substituting I (instructor) for A, and F (fencer) for B.

Both fencers are in full gear. B is at middle distance from A's wrist.

1. *A moves back and forth while engaging B's blade in 6th position. A stops and opens line. B extends arm and hits A's wrist with a short advance.*
2. *A applies slight pressure in 6th position. B disengages, extends, and hits A's inside wrist with a short advance.*
3. *A executes beat 6. B beats back in 6th, extends, and hits A on the outside wrist with a short advance.*
4. *As in #1, #2, and #3 above, A presents the same cues in 4th line.*
5. *As in #1, #2, #3, and #4 above, B hits with a lunge rather than an advance, as A steps back.*

Thrust-in-Opposition

In épée fencing, thrusts must be executed with an opposition in order to neutralize the opponent's counterattack or stop-thrust. The opposition-thrust begins with absence of contact with the opponent's blade, blocking the opponent's counterattack.

To be fully effective, the closing of the line in opposition must occur on the final movement of the thrust.

Thrust with Opposition 4 in Short Distance

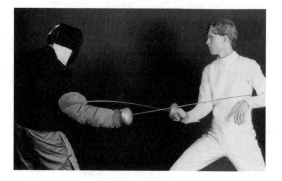

Thrust with Opposition 5
to the Flank in Short
Distance

Drills for Thrust-in-Opposition

The following drills are for instructor (I) and fencer (F):

I leads, engaging F's blade in 4th line. F is at middle distance from the crook of I's arm:

1. *I leads back and forth, stops, opens line. F executes the straight thrust with a short lunge to the crook of I's arm, closing the line at the last moment. (After the initial cue of opening the line, I should start extending the arm slowly, initiating a counterattack.)*
2. *As in #1 above, the thrust is to I's chest. The distance between I and F must be lengthened to adjust to the new target.*
3. *As in #2 above, flèche to the chest followed by immediate remise.*

The Flick (Cutover)

The "flick" is similar to a coupé or cutover, but on a smaller scale. It is executed with a quick, "snapping" upward and downward action of the wrist, causing the blade to curve over the opponent's bell guard, thereby placing the point on the opponent's hand, wrist, or forearm.

The flick is used to score a touch, to provoke the counterattack, and to disturb, distract, or deter the opponent. It is accomplished by a sharp up and down movement of the hand in 6th, 3rd, 2nd, or 8th position.

Drills for the Flick

The following drills are for instructor (I) and fencer (F). The instructor may adjust the drills according to the skill level of the fencer.

F is at short distance from I's forearm. F engages I's blade in 8th position.

1. *F starts the action from 8th position, executes two flicks on I's hand or wrist, follows with a short lunge to I's shoulder.*

2. I advances. F executes two flicks to I's hand or wrist. I continues to advance while raising the blade in 6th position. F executes the lunge backward with thrust to I's knee, takes I's blade in 6th position, and hits I's chest with a glide-flèche attack following with a remise.

3. F executes two flicks to I's hand or wrist and returns to engagement in 8th position. I attempts to hit F's forearm with a straight thrust. F parries 6 and ripostes with the flick to I's forearm, with a remise to the chest.

4. I walks forward slowly. F executes two flicks while retreating, returns to engagement in 8th position.

Continue this exercise for the entire length of the strip.

At end of the strip, I presents the blade in F's outside line. F parries 6th, hits I's chest with the flèche, and follows with a remise.

5. From erect and stationary position. F executes two flicks to I's hand or wrist, point remaining near I's hand. I attempts to engage F's blade in 4th line. F pronates hand under I's blade and executes flick to I's outside wrist. I presents blade on F's outside line; F lifts hand into 6th position and raises I's blade with thrust to I's shoulder or chest.

6. As in #5 above, with I advancing.

7. From erect position, F executes two flicks to I's hand or wrist, point remaining near I's hand. I attempts to engage F's blade in 4th line while stepping forward. F while retreating, executes disengage thrust to crook of I's arm. On completion of the retreat, F parries 6th followed by glide-flèche to I's chest, and remise.

8. From standing position, F executes two flicks on I's hand or wrist with point remaining near I's hand. I attempts to engage F's blade in 4th line. F pronates his or her hand under I's blade, executes flick to I's low outside line on hand or wrist. I then attempts to take F's blade in 6th line. F supinates hand under I's blade, executing flick to I's low inside line on hand or wrist.

Blade Control

To score a touch, the épée fencer must rely on speed and accuracy, therefore blade control is of utmost importance.

Actions executed on the opponent's blade are very common in épée fencing. They give the fencer the opportunity to neutralize the opponent's counterattack, remise, or stop-thrust. Furthermore, they reduce the chances of a double touch—an important factor when the opponent is leading in the score.

The beginning fencer must learn to determine when an action on the blade is more appropriate than an action without blade contact. This helps a fencer develop a general strategy against the opponent. Which action is chosen will depend on the distance separating the opponents, the position of the opponent's blade and on the score of the bout at the time. The first factors involve such technical considerations as

(1) whether to execute a beat or attack with absence of blade contact, or maintain control of the opponent's blade throughout the action; or (2) execute a glide rather than a transfer of the blade to another line.

The score of the bout at the time presents certain tactical issues for consideration—for example:

When to attempt a double-touch.
How to score a double-touch.
When to avoid a double-touch.
How to avoid a double-touch.
How to attack and score without taking the opponent's blade.
How to select the proper target.

Drills for Blade Control

The following drills are for instructor (I) and fencer (F):

F is at long distance from I.
1. *F advances and engages I's blade in 4th position. I disengages, presenting blade on F's outside line. F parries 6th and lunges with a glide in 6th to I's shoulder or chest.*
2. *F advances, engages I's blade in 4th position. I disengages with a lunge to F's chest. F executes a strong beat parry 6th with riposte to I's flank, followed by a remise.*
3. *F advances, engages I's blade in 4th position. I disengages with a flèche to F's chest. F executes a strong beat-parry 6th with riposte to I's flank.*
4. *F advances, engages I's blade in 6th position. I disengages with a lunge. F executes a stop thrust to I's arm, followed by a beat-parry on the retreat, with riposte to I's arm upon completion of the retreat.*
5. *F advances, engages I's blade in 6th position. I disengages, presenting the blade with a flexed arm, on F's inside line. F parries 4th, lunges with a glide to the crook of the arm, shoulder, or chest.*
6. *F advances, engages I's blade in 6th position. I disengages, presenting the blade with the arm fully extended; F takes the blade in 4th, transfers (binds) to 8th, and lunges to I's hip, thigh, foot, or flank, according to the distance.*
7. *F advances, engages I's blade in 6th position. I disengages, presenting the blade with the arm fully extended. F takes the blade in 4th, changes engagement back to 6th, transfers (binds) to high 7th line, lunges with a glide to I's flank. (Note: In #6 and #7, F may step back when taking the blade in 4th.)*
8. *F advances, engages I's blade in 4th position. I, with arm slightly flexed, disengages, then presents blade on F's outside line. F parries 6th, lunges with glide to crook of arm, shoulder, or outside chest area.*
9. *In all the above drills, F may complete the action with a flèche, followed by a quick remise.*

These drills for blade control are designed to teach:

Proper coordination of weapon-arm and leg movements.

When to execute a glide, a transfer, or an envelopment (circular transfer) according to the distance and the position of the opponent's blade and the movement of the opponent on the strip.

A beginning student should execute these and other drills slowly. Speed will come naturally after the proper coordination has been mastered. To facilitate the learning process, the instructor should focus primarily on blade control drills without footwork. For example:

1. *F is in short distance from I's arm. F takes the blade in 6th position (I's arm is flexed), envelopes the blade several times in 6th, and hits I's crook of the arm with a final envelopment. It is important that the final envelopment is executed in progression toward the target—that is, that the blade is constantly spiralling toward the target, culminating in the final thrust.*
2. *As in #1 above, while F is enveloping the blade in 6th position, I extends the arm. F must transfer (bind) the blade to high 7th during the final thrust.*
3. *As in #1 and #2 above, F starts in 4th. Accordingly, the envelopment will return the blade to the 4th position, the transfer (bind) will culminate on the outside low line.*
4. *As in #1, #2, and #3 above, I moves forward slowly, and F executes these drills while retreating. If F transfers (binds) I's blade, the final touch is executed with a lunge or a step forward.*

These drills can also be executed by fencers in pairs.

TACTICAL DEVELOPMENT

Épée fencing is not governed by the rule of right-of-way. Consequently, in épée it is easier to counterattack than to attack.

The novice épée fencer must develop an understanding of the tactical aspects of the game as soon as possible. The technique necessary to implement the tactical game will be acquired through time and practice. Because épée fencing requires extreme precision and superb point control, the épée fencer should spend as much time as possible on drills that develop, enhance, and refine proper point control.

An understanding of the tactical game usually inspires and motivates the fencer to improve the technical skills that are necessary for implementing the proper strategies. Once the fencer understands basic tactical concepts, he or she will gradually become aware of the many tactical problems inherent in épée fencing and spontaneously find solutions to them. Therefore, it is advisable to devote as much time as possible to bouting.

All fencers should learn the structure and format relative to official competitive bouts. For details on this subject, see Chapter 2, on foil fencing.

LEARNING EXPERIENCE—BEGINNING TACTICAL BOUTS

The following drills use electrical scoring apparatus.

1. Fencer A wants to provoke Fencer B's counterattack by advancing and executing a flick on B's wrist or hand. B counterattacks to A's hand. A completes the action with a glide lunge to score.
2. As in #1 above, B fakes the counterattack to A's hand and avoids A's attempt to take the blade by using disengage. (Vary this drill with #1 above.)
3. If B does not counterattack, A has the choice of completing the attack, on or off the blade, to any open target.
4. A is given the option to execute a direct attack in lieu of the flick.
5. A provokes B's counterattack by faking a beat attack. A executes a quick beat followed by a short thrust aimed at B's hand or forearm. B executes a counterattack to A's arm. A takes B's blade in opposition and completes the action.
6. B has the option of faking the counterattack and disengaging A's subsequent attempt of engagement.
7. If B does not counterattack, A completes the attack.
8. A has the option of executing a direct attack in lieu of the fake beat attack. The direct attack may be executed off the blade to any target, including the foot, or the blade with a glide-thrust.
9. A wishes to provoke B's counterattack by applying quick pressure on B's blade on the 4th line. B counterattacks with a disengage. A takes the blade and completes the attack or executes a thrust in opposition.
10. B has the option of executing a feint-disengage counterattack. A should stop-hit on B's arm.
11. If B does not counterattack, A has the option of finishing the attack with the first engagement in 4th.
12. A has the option of executing a direct glide-thrust or faking an attack.
13. As in #9 through #12 above, employ pressure in 6th position.

These drills on beginning tactics will help the fencer learn:

How to draw the counterattack.
How to execute a false attack.
How to vary a false attack with a real attack.
To recognize a false attack.
What to do against a false attack.
To take advantage of an opponent's slow reaction.

The instructor should refrain from making any corrections while the fencers practice these drills. The tactics of the drill should be freely interpreted by the fencers and incorporated in the bout. Only during the lesson should the instructor address areas that are deficient with regard to comprehension and execution.

Even during the lesson, the instructor should hold corrections to a minimum, while encouraging the fencer to develop his or her own style. Accordingly, the fencer should be allowed to assume his or her own preferred guard position. This allows the fencer to move comfortably on the strip without undue influence from various "authorities."

It is important for the beginner to recognize that the score of the bout at the moment generally dictates the strategy to use. Therefore, the fencer should always be aware of the score differential.

Lesson Drill for Tactics

In the following drills, two fencers (A and B), the instructor, a stopwatch, and full electrical gear are needed. Fencer A is leading 4 to 3 with 1 minute remaining.

1. Fencer A should attempt to effect a double-touch; B should avoid a double-touch.
2. The instructor may vary the score and the time remaining, thus creating different tactical situations. Also, the instructor may have the fencers start the drill at the center of the strip or at each end.

Technique and Tactics

In combat, technique cannot be separated from tactics, and neither can the physical and psychological aspects of the competitive bout be separated. The fencer who is familiar with all possible offensive, counteroffensive, and defensive moves can develop the tactics required for competition. In other words, a fencer's tactics depend on having a rich arsenal of fencing actions.

The outcome of any combat is affected by the training and skill of the athlete who has adequate tactical-technical preparation, physical conditioning, stamina, coordinated reflexes, and self-control. Tactical abilities are acquired through drills, lessons, and bouts. It is the instructor's responsibility to stimulate the tactical development of the fencer by offering the fencers increasingly complex tactical situations.

In fencing, it is the understanding of tactics, not just the common knowledge of the technical moves and tactics, that distinguishes a successful fencer from an average fencer.

HIGHLIGHTS

1. Name three schools that helped competitive épée fencing to grow.
2. Name the founder(s) of épée schools from two different countries.
3. Which school may be considered the modern "factory" for developing épée fencers?
4. What decision is rendered on a double-touch in épée?
5. May a referee annul a registered touch? If so, when?

6. Within what time frame in electrical épée fencing is a double-touch scored?
7. Describe the target area in épée fencing.
8. Define what is meant by the "advanced target" area.
9. Define the "central target" area.
10. Demonstrate lunging forward with recovery to the rear.
11. Demonstrate lunging backward with recovery to the rear.
12. After attacking opponent with a lunge, when is a fencer most vulnerable?
13. To avoid being vulnerable to the opponent, what may a fencer choose to do from the lunge position?
14. Describe and demonstrate the execution of "small jumps."
15. Demonstrate the jump forward and the balestra.
16. Describe the steps taken to execute the advance.
17. Describe the steps taken to execute the retreat.
18. Describe and demonstrate the flèche from the on-guard position and from the lunge position.
19. Demonstrate the straight thrust at short distance.
20. Demonstrate the thrust-lunge at middle distance.
21. With an advance from middle distance, demonstrate hitting the opponent's wrist with the straight thrust.
22. Execute a disengage against an opponent's blade pressure in 6th position, and hit the inside of the opponent's wrist.
23. Differentiate between thrust in opposition and glide thrust.
24. Explain the tactical basis for blade control.

Jana Angelakis, Three-Time
U.S. National Champion

5

Strategy

The basic strategy in fencing is (a) to hit the opponent while avoiding being hit and (b), in foil and saber, to hit the opponent while enjoying protection of the right-of-way rule.

DEVELOPING STRATEGY

A fencer should have a plan of action before approaching the fencing strip. At the end of the bout, it is good practice to review and analyze the action.

To develop strategy for bouting, a fencer should first learn the fundamental skills of fencing, know and be able to apply the rules of fencing, acquire the stamina for fencing, and know fencing protocol.

Master the Basic Skills

The first step in developing strategy is to master the fundamental skills. A beginner is eager to cross blades and bout. Many instructors permit this early in the learning stage to illustrate that learning fundamental skills is essential to success. Most instructors insist that experienced fencers as well as beginners include a review of fundamentals in their daily program.

Continual improvement leading to mastery of basic skills is an integral part of any fencing program. When the fencer's execution of fundamentals becomes conditioned reflexes, complete attention can then be centered on the plan of action, or strategy. Controlled movements can be made only if the movements have been mastered. Lack of control leads to irrational actions. Fencing requires stamina, and unnecessary expenditure of energy can lead to early fatigue. Executing movements correctly will conserve energy by avoiding wasted motion.

Mastery of fundamentals provides the foundation on which to build a repertoire of actions. All compound fencing phrases are merely a series of simple moves made in proper sequence, time, and distance. Unless these simple movements are first mastered, a fencer cannot hope to execute complex actions successfully.

Know and Apply the Rules

The second step is to learn, understand, and apply the rules of fencing. Rules are designed to create a safe, suitable, and equitable bouting environment. Ignorance of rules results in uncertainty and insecurity. For example, Fencer A has initiated an attack that strikes the opponent on a valid target, and Fencer B also scores. The referee (formerly director or president) declares a touch against A. If the rule of right-of-way is misunderstood, the fencer may not comprehend the decision. What A may have believed was an effective attack was not deemed so by the referee. A may now hesitate to use that attack—or any attack—again.

Ignorance is no excuse for violating fencing rules. Fencers are bound by the rules and regulations governing competitions in which they compete. The official rules for divisional, sectional, and national competitions (in the United States) are based on the international rules and are published periodically by the United States Fencing Association. College and university conferences operate under slightly modified USFA rules. These modifications usually relate to the time limits and structure of competitions. The rules governing the validity of hits are the same worldwide.

Develop Endurance and Stamina

The third step is to develop endurance and stamina. In a competition of short duration, endurance may be less important than skill and technique, but its importance becomes obvious in extended competitions.

The body will perform more efficiently if given proper care. Both physical conditioning and skills training are imperative for developing fencing ability. The former involves exercise, proper diet, adequate sleep, and abstinence from drugs, smoking, and alcoholic beverages. The latter refers to the development of fencing skills through regular instruction and practice.

Learn the Protocol

The fourth step is to learn the protocol of the sport. By observing protocol, a fencer earns the respect of opponents, officials, and spectators.

A fencer who can answer yes to the following questions has learned fencing protocol:

Do you dress properly in clean fencing clothes?

Do you have an extra weapon and an extra body cord handy in case of a break down, so time will not be wasted?

Do you offer to help hook up the electrical equipment? Score? Time? Judge?

Are you ready to fence when your bout is called?

Do you salute your opponent before the bout begins and shake hands at the conclusion of the bout?

Do you know how to request time out?

Do you thank the officials at the conclusion of a match?

DEVELOPING TACTICAL COMPETENCE

To further enhance fencing strategy, tactical competence must be developed.

Learn to Think Analytically

Acquiring tactical competence requires an understanding and personal assessment of one's abilities. Some fencers never learn to rely upon their own judgment and must be told what to do and when to do it. A fencer should learn to think analytically by doing the following:

Recognize your strengths and weaknesses and try to capitalize on them. Use defensive maneuvers that have proven to be most successful. For example, an aggressive competitor should emphasize attacks but be ready to parry and counterattack.

An extremely cautious fencer should strengthen his or her defense by using ripostes and counter-time actions.

Be aware of possible responses to an action. Each opponent will react to a threat in one of three ways: by retreating, by attacking, or by holding ground. If the opponent retreats, the response may be to pursue and score. If the opponent attacks, the response may be either to stop-hit or to parry and riposte. If the opponent is holding ground, the response may be attack to score. If the attack is not successful, be prepared to execute a secondary action.

Know various tactics that force the opponent to readjust and reassess strategy. It is advisable to probe the opponent with feints directed at all lines in order to seek out normal responses. If a particular action is scoring, continue to use it. As soon as you anticipate that an action will fail to score, attempt a different action—but return to the original action later in the bout.

Develop self-confidence. A fencer must be willing to take some risks in order to score, but once the decision to take a calculated risk is made should be totally committed to that action, believing it will succeed. An opponent frequently feels threatened as much by a fencer's confidence as by the weapon point.

Learn to control the distance. To avoid being hit by an opponent's attack, a fencer may employ three methods: (a) deflect the blade from the target, (b) remove the target by retreating or advancing, or (c) use a combination of both. Some fencers require a great distance for coordinating a smooth, composed attack, and also depend on the opponent's retreating. Occasionally, to abort an attack, a fencer should hold ground as the opponent advances. This not only decreases the distance required but also interrupts the tempo.

Few fencers feel comfortable when they are at the end of the strip, yet this location can be used to advantage if overeagerness causes the opponent to miscalculate the distance. Good balance and position are part of distance control. It is of no benefit to be at the right distance or to use the correct move at the appropriate time if lack of balance prevents scoring.

Develop a feeling for tempo. Every fencing movement has a rhythm (cadence) that can be used to advantage by either fencer. For example, many fencers try to mesmerize the opponent by making slow, hypnotic movements with the weapon to establish a rhythm.

At the right moment the fencer strikes with decisiveness and rapidity, and the opponent is scored on before he or she is able to react. To avoid becoming the victim of such mesmerism, vary the pace of the movements so the opponent is unable to find a pattern to the tempo. Reversing the above example may sometimes be effective. By making quick, staccato movements, you will lead the opponent to expect a lightning-fast attack. Find an opening and score by making a slower, more deliberate attack.

Learn to Assess the Opponent

The next step in acquiring tactical competence is to learn to understand and assess the opponent. A fencer must be aware that the opponent will change strategy from time to time. Watch the opponent bout with others, and observe any habits or patterns. It is easier to take advantage of these than to force a change. Determine:

The opponent's distance.

Whether the opponent's parries are controlled and well conceived and whether the blade can be deceived.

How much distance the opponent covers when lunging and how quickly the lunge and recovery are executed.

Whether the opponent gives away any attack movements—for example, do the fingers of the trailing hand wiggle? does the shoulder droop? is the on-guard position deepened just before attacking?

Each situation calls for a slightly different response. The greater a fencer's experience and knowledge, the more intelligent the response will be. Regard the opponent as a puzzle to be solved in the fewest possible movements.

The attacker usually has greater opportunity to score than the defender, so, the attacking strategy becomes clear—press the opponent with attacks, and attack with vigor and decisive commitment. Hesitation may lose the right-of-way. It is advisable to be unpredictable, varying the attacks so there will be no discernible pattern.

Learn to Understand and Assess the Officials

The third step in acquiring tactical competence is to understand and assess the officials (the referee and the judges). Many a disgruntled fencer has walked off a strip defeated, failing to understand the referee's decisions.

Learn to listen to the referee's interpretations of fencing actions and use this information to plan tactics. To avoid doubtful touches or simultaneous actions, score in such a way that there can be no question about who has the right-of-way.

Avoid showing anger or disgust on the strip. The officials and the spectators may take this as a sign of disrespect. A wise fencer will not discuss a decision with the opponent during or immediately after a bout.

Learn to Understand and Assess the Environment

The fourth step in acquiring tactical competence is to understand and assess the physical environment, which is generally beyond a fencer's control. Awareness of physical factors that might affect performance will prepare the fencer to cope with them. A fencer should determine the following:

Is the lighting better on one end of the strip than on the other?

Are the strips too close to one another? Is sufficient end space allowed? Are there any physical obstructions?

Are conditions satisfactory for executing a flèche attack?

Of what material is the fencing surface made? Does it provide suitable traction?

Is the audience apt to be partisan and vocal?

Is the room temperature comfortable for competitors?
If electrical apparatus is being used, have the reels, body cords, and other equipment been checked?

LEARNING EXPERIENCE—SUGGESTED RESPONSES TO FENCING SITUATIONS

1. *Each opponent will exhibit some habitual characteristics. The list below is in no way exhaustive, but it provides suggested responses to some specific situations.*
    The bout has just started:
        a. Recognize the habitual parries of the opponent by using false attacks to expose his or her reactions.
        b. Note the speed of the opponent's movements.
        c. Judge the distance of the opponent by inviting attacks.
    The opponent has a low guard:
        a. Attack to high line.
        b. Feint high, hit low on reaction.
        c. Beat blade, attack high.
    The opponent maintains an extended arm:
        a. Beat.
        b. Take-the-blade.
    The opponent habitually employs the stop-thrust:
        a. Perform simple attacks.
        b. Attack with action on the blade.
        c. False attack, parry the stop-hit, riposte (counter-time).
    The opponent offers invitations:
        a. Extend and advance with caution until opponent returns to on-guard.
        b. Feint, then deceive opponent's attempt to contact the blade.
        c. Use simple attack only if in distance.
    The opponent does not respond to feints:
        a. Perform simple attack with all-out effort.
        b. Seek reactions to actions on the blade.
        c. Invite attack, and parry riposte.
    The opponent is of short stature:
        a. Stay out of the opponent's reach.
        b. Use stop-hits.
    The opponent is of tall stature:
        a. Gain distance cautiously.
        b. Use aggressive actions on the blade.
        c. Use attacks of second intention.
        d. Move into distance to fence at close quarters.
    The opponent has a weak defense:
        a. Use varied attacks.
        b. False attack, remise, or reprise.
        c. Use redoublement.

The opponent is left-handed:
  a. *Draw the opponent into the 4th position and deceive the circular parry 4.*
  b. *Finish your attacks in opponent's outside lines.*
  c. *Feint low outside, hit high.*
  d. *Attack with a change beat-6-cutover.*

2. *Observe an intercollegiate, national, or club competition. What offensive techniques were employed? What style of defense was used? Were counteractions used? How were these various actions executed?*
3. *Observe the techniques employed by the referee. Does the referee know the rules? Were the calls consistent? Was the bout kept under control? How would you evaluate the referee's performance?*
4. *Keep a notebook in which you describe and analyze the styles and actions of your opponents.*
5. *At the conclusion of each bout, record how each fencer scored and determine appropriate countermovements. Also record the strategy employed to score.*

HIGHLIGHTS

1. Explain the basic strategy of fencing.
2. Explain how basic skills, rules, and protocol are related to strategy.
3. List the advantages to be gained by thoroughly learning the fundamental skills.
4. Explain the effect of endurance and stamina.
5. What organization publishes the rules of fencing?
6. List five rules of protocol a fencer should observe.
7. Describe how you would respond to an opponent who retreats, attacks, or holds ground.
8. Describe three maneuvers to avoid a hit.
9. Explain how fencing distance can be used to advantage.
10. In developing strategy, what steps can be taken to assess yourself, the opponent, the officials, and the environment?

6

The Rules of Competition

Fencing competitions are governed by rules designed to ensure equity and the safety of each participant. The rules of fencing, which are the framework for applying skills and knowledge, are presented in condensed form in this chapter. It is the prerogative of the Fédération Internationale d'Escrime (FIE) to alter and revise the rules based on technological advances and increased number of participants, to further spectator appeal, to accommodate media coverage, and to improve safety measures. Therefore, it behooves every reader and participant to keep abreast of the latest rule changes published by the United States Fencing Association (USFA).

Unabridged rules and regulations governing conventional and electrical fencing are listed in the current edition of the United States Fencing Association rules book.

The Fencing Guide of the National Association for Girls and Women in Sport also includes the rules and interpretations. (Today's rules for foil fencing are basically the same as those adopted in 1914 in Paris. The rules having to do with electrical apparatus and equipment were adopted in 1957.) "Ignorance of the rules is no excuse," according to the official rules. Therefore, each fencer should become completely familiar with the rules through study and competition.

FENCING BOUT BOUNDARIES

A fencing bout is held on a strip of regulation size. The piste (strip or mat) measures between 1.8 meters (5 feet 11 inches) and 2 meters (6 feet 7 inches) in width and is 14 meters (45 feet 11 inches) long. End zones or safety zones extend 1.5 to 2 meters (4 feet 11 inches to 6 feet 7 inches) on each end of the strip, making the total length of advisable space for competition 17 to 18 meters (55 feet 9 inches to 59 feet).

A fencer is required to bout within the boundaries of the strip. Certain conventions govern crossing the end and side boundaries:

1. If a fencer crosses the end line of the strip with both feet, the referee (formerly called "president" or "director") will halt the bout and award the touch for the opponent.
2. When a fencer crosses the lateral (side) boundary of the strip with one foot, the referee halts the bout, ordering that fencer on-guard at the point where he or she crossed the lateral boundary line. No penalty is imposed.
3. When a fencer crosses with both feet, the touch if scored by this fencer while being off the strip is illegal and nullified and the opponent is instructed to move forward 1 meter.

Bout Officials

A fencing bout is under the control of the referee assisted by four judges (in absence of a scoring apparatus), a scorekeeper, and a timekeeper.

The referee decides the validity or priority of a hit; the judges determine the materiality of a hit. In electrical fencing, the electrical scoring device replaces the four judges. In foil, even with the use of electrical scoring apparatus, it is sometimes necessary to call on two side judges, whose responsibility it is each to observe an opponent to ensure that no infraction of the rule is committed, such as covering a valid target with an invalid target (for example, using the trailing arm). In foil and épée the two side judges may also be called on to watch for touches being registered by hitting an object off the metallic strip. The scorekeeper and timekeeper are adjunct personnel assisting the referee.

Before a bout begins, the scorekeeper announces the names of the opponents according to a prescribed order. The fencer whose name is called first by the scorekeeper stands behind the guard line to the right of the referee, except when the first-called is left-handed and the opponent is right-handed.

The referee gives the order "On Guard!" then asks "Ready?" If the fencers respond affirmatively, or in absence of a negative reply, the referee orders "Fence!" Then the bout officially begins. The fencers continue bouting until the referee calls "Halt!" Play is resumed in the middle of the strip after a touch is scored, and at the same place where it is halted if no touch is scored. When using nonelectric weapons, fencers change sides after one fencer has scored half the maximum number of hits— that is, three. In electrical fencing, fencers do not change sides.

Scoring

The immediate goal of bouting is to score legal hits (touches). For thrusting weapons—foil and épée—a hit is scored when the point of the weapon arrives on a valid target. For foil, the target is the trunk of the body, including the groin area, plus the collar area in the front, and the collar to the hip joints in the rear; the bib of the mask is not part of the target. For épée, the valid target is the entire body, including arms, legs, and head. In saber, a touch may be scored by thrusting with the point or cutting the target area, which includes entire body above the hipline, including the arms and head.

The Rule of Right-of-Way

The fundamental principle of scoring hits for foil and saber fencing is the rule of right-of-way. This rule is employed by the referee in determining the validity and priority of a hit when both fencers are hit at approximately the same instant.

Generally speaking, the rule states that a fencer, initiating an aggressive action in which the weapon arm is moving forward and threatening the opponent's target has the right-of-way until the opponent defends and ripostes. Then the opponent has the right-of-way. If the opponent fails to parry and initiate an attack, or after parrying hesitates before riposting, the original attacker may resume the attack and thus retake the right-of-way. When the two fencers are hit at the end of the same phrase, only the first hit scores, if there is a discernible difference in time. But if the difference in time is slight, the hit having the right-of-way scores, even if it arrives slightly after the other hit. In foil, if the two hits arrive at approximately the same time, it is deemed that neither has the right-of-way, and no touch is awarded. In saber, the decision, in the event of simultaneous attacks, with both landing on valid target, results in a double touch—a point for each fencer.

The winner of a bout is the person who first scores a predetermined number of hits within a set time. A variety of bouts are employed in fencing competitions, such as the basic 5-touch bouts for pools; 10-touch bouts, 15-touch bouts—namely, three 5-touch encounters for matches of direct elimination tables.

In épée there is no right-of-way rule. The fencer who scores the hit first receives a touch. If both fencers score at the same time, it is called a double-touch and both fencers add 1 point to their score.

Time Limit

The duration of a bout in official USFA competitions is four minutes of actual fencing time (the time between the orders "Fence" and "Halt") for a basic five-touch bout. When the time limit expires before five touches have been scored by one fencer, the following apply:

If one fencer has scored more hits than the opponent has, the number of hits required must be added to the score to bring it up to five, and the same number of hits must be added to the opponent's score.

If both fencers have received the maximum number of hits, they are both regarded as having received the maximum number of hits being fought for, and a victory with a score of V:4 is awarded to the higher-ranked fencer. Ranks of both fencers must be determined before the bout has started. In other words, in any bout, if the score is tied at 5-all before the final touch, the double touch is not awarded and the fencers retain their position on the strip and continue with the bout until time runs out. In the event of a tied score, the referee will determine in advance by lot, for bouts in a pool, which fencer is the winner when time runs out. (There will be no more double defeats in épée.)

For direct elimination bouts, the referee will announce which fencer had the higher seed in the initial table and will therefore be the winner of the bout should it end in a tie when time runs out. If there is a tie in the seeding into the table, the referee will determine by lot, and announce before the bout starts, which fencer will be the winner of the bout should time run out.

Penalties

By adhering to USFA rules for competition, one may well avoid many unnecessary penalties. Infractions of the rules and conduct of fencing carry penalties that range from loss of ground on the strip (as incurred when crossing the strip boundaries) to expulsion from the competition (as might occur in certain cases of unsportsmanlike conduct). The referee and the Bout Committee are obliged to expel from the site of the competition, with or without prior warning, any fencer, spectator, coach, supporter, attendant, auxiliary person, or official who by gesture, attitude, or word disturbs the smooth running of the competition.

The 1990 revised USFA Penalty Chart summarizes the many offenses and their penalties. References for the penalties are listed in parentheses by number on the chart and may be found in the USFA rules manual, which provides information in detail.

OFFENSES	ARTICLES	Penalty Cards: 1st 2nd 3rd + Offense		
		1st call YC	2nd call RC	3rd call BC
Not present to fence on time (3 calls at 1 min intervals)[5]	604, 650			

First Group:

OFFENSES	ARTICLES			
Non-conforming equipment,[1] no spare regulation weapon, no national armband (official FIE competitions)	21, 27	Y E L L O W C A R D	R E D C A R D	R E D C A R D
Voluntary corps à corps (and involuntary - F,S), jostling, falling, disorderly fencing, reversing shoulders (F)[2]	28, 34, 224 318, 412			
Raising the mask before the President's decision	28			
Covering or substitution of valid target (F,S)	30, 411			
Using the non-weapon arm or hand[2]	30			
Touching/holding the electrical equipment	30			
Leaving the strip without permission	32			
Turning the back on the opponent[2]	35			
Crossing the side of the strip to avoid a touch	43			
Delaying the bout	48			
Placing the point of the weapon on the strip (F, E)	211, 316			
Grounding the weapon on the lamé (F)[2]	230			
Voluntary touch not on the opponent (F,E)	230, 325			
Touch scored with the guard (S)[2]	409			
Disobedience	602f., 606, 609			
Unjustified appeal	661			

Second Group:

OFFENSES	ARTICLES			
Absence of inspection marks[1,3]	21	R E D	R E D	R E D
Violent, dangerous or vindictive act, hit with guard or pommel[2]	28			
Unjustified claim of injury[4]	50			
Voluntary touch not on the opponent **in final minute** (F,E)	230, 325			

Third Group:

OFFENSES	ARTICLES			
Falsified inspection marks, modification of equipment[1,3,4,5]	21	R E D	B L A C K	
Dishonest fencing[2,5]	28			
Fencer disturbing order on the strip[5,8]	602			
Offense concerning publicity code[5]	PC			
Anyone disturbing order off the strip (1st: warning; 2nd: expulsion)[7,8]	602			

Fourth Group:

OFFENSES	ARTICLES			
Obvious fraud in the equipment[1,2,4,6]	21	B L A C K		
Intentional brutality[2,5]	28			
Unsportsmanlike conduct[2,5/6]	605			
Favoring the opponent, profiting from collusion[5]	607			
Doping[6]	608			

YELLOW = WARNING / RED = PENALTY TOUCH / BLACK = EXCLUSION

[1] Confiscation of non-conforming equipment
[2] Annulment of touch scored by fencer at fault
[3] Annulment of last touch scored by fencer at fault, even if fencing has recommenced
[4] Consult medical/technical experts
[5] Exclusion from the competition
[6] Exclusion from the tournament
[7] Expulsion from the site of the competition
[8] In the most severe cases, the President may exclude or expel the offender immediately.

A fencer cannot receive a YELLOW CARD after receiving any RED CARD in the same bout. A fencer does not receive a 3rd group BLACK CARD without already having received a 3rd group RED CARD in that bout.

USFA Penalty Chart

LEARNING EXPERIENCE—UNDERSTANDING THE RULES

1. *Observe a fencing competition to note the application of various fencing rules. Question experienced referees on the nuances of rule interpretations.*
2. *Refer to other strategies that deal with rules. This will expand your understanding and application of the rules.*
3. *Refer to the USFA rules manual for further refinements.*

HIGHLIGHTS

1. Describe a fencing strip, giving its dimensions and stating the purposes of the lines on the strip.
2. State the penalties for crossing both the lateral and end boundaries of a strip.
3. List the officials and state each one's main responsibility.
4. Describe the orderly sequence for starting a bout.
5. Explain how the winner is determined.
6. Explain how a tie is resolved.
7. Explain the rule of right-of-way.

7

Officiating

Officiating is a skill acquired through study, observation, and experience. Despite the need for developing competent officials, officiating is a most neglected aspect of fencing. Classes, clinics, and workshops can help develop a better understanding of the basic rules and increase skill in the techniques and mechanics of officiating.

Learning to officiate should be a part of every beginner's training because it helps fencers understand how decisions are made and because fencers are often called on to officiate.

OFFICIATING SKILLS

A fencer should develop the skills and personal characteristics that are necessary for officiating:

Knowledge, interpretation, and application of rules.
Prompt reaction—registering decisions quickly.
Self-confidence.

Consistency in judgment—recognizing the significance of every action, being unbiased, and registering the same decisions for instances exactly alike.

Creditable behavior—developing self-control in order to establish and maintain rapport with fencers, coaches, officials, and spectators.

A well-groomed physical appearance.

Good physical condition, in order to move with the action.

Successful application of these characteristics is often affected by the referee's style in controlling the bout with as little interference as possible.

THE OFFICIALS

When using conventional (nonelectrical) equipment, the officiating jury includes a referee and four judges. Other officials are a scorekeeper and a timekeeper.

The Referee

The referee (until only recently called the president or director) has complete control over the fencers, coaches, officials, and spectators. The referee's duties are to award hits according to the rules, to see that order is maintained, to observe the actions of both fencers, and to interpret these actions to the judges clearly.

The Judges

The judges are responsible for determining whether or not a hit has been made.

Two of the judges (Judges 1 and 2 in the illustration) are on the referee's right to observe hits against the fencer on the referee's left. Judges 3 and 4 observe hits on the opposing fencer.

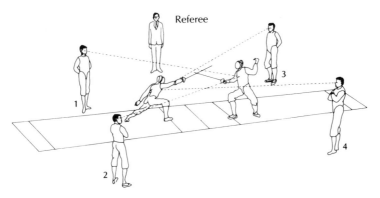

Positioning of Officials

The judges assume positions around the strip and the fencers without interfering with the action. To ensure safety, they stand about 3 feet (1 meter) from the edge of the strip and 3 feet behind the nearest competitor. They move with the competitors to ensure an unobstructed view of the action and assigned target.

As soon as a judge observes an invalid (off-target) hit on the fencer he or she is watching, the judge must immediately raise an arm overhead to advise the referee, who will halt the bout. If necessary, the referee briefly reconstructs the actions of the last fencing phrase before the call "Halt," analyzes them, and asks the judges for their opinions. The judges must reply promptly and decisively by voting one of the following: (1) "Yes." (2) "Off target." (3) "No." (4) "I abstain." The referee votes last.

The opinion of each judge counts as one vote, while the referee's opinion has a value of 1½ votes. By abstaining, an official indicates uncertainty, and consequently there is no point value.

LEARNING EXPERIENCE

Fencer A attacks Fencer B. Judges 1 and 2, watching B, raise their arms. The referee halts the bout. Reviewing the action, the referee asks: "The attack?" Judges 1 and 2 vote "Yes." What is the decision? (B is hit.)

If the judges on the same end (1 and 2, or 3 and 4) agree (by saying "Yes," "No," or "Off target"), their judgment prevails.

LEARNING EXPERIENCE

Fencer A attacks Fencer B. Judge 1 raises an arm. The referee halts the bout. Reviewing the action, the referee asks: "The attack?" Judge 1 votes "Yes." Judge 2 votes "I abstain." The referee votes "No." What is the decision? (No score.)

If one of the judges has a definite opinion and the other abstains, the opinion of the referee, whose vote is overriding, prevails. If the referee also abstains, the decision of the judge with a definite opinion prevails.

LEARNING EXPERIENCE

Fencer A attacks Fencer B. Judge 1 raises an arm. The referee halts the bout. Reviewing the action, the referee asks: "The attack?" Judge 1 votes "Yes." Judge 2 votes "No." The referee votes "I abstain." What is the decision? (Doubtful hit or benefit of the doubt—no score.)

If the two judges at the same end (1 and 2, or 3 and 4) are positive but have contrary opinions or if both abstain, the referee casts the determining vote. If the referee also abstains, the hit is regarded as doubtful and there is no score. A doubtful hit is never scored against a competitor. Also, any hit must be annulled if made subsequently or simultaneously in the same phrase by the fencer receiving the benefit of the doubt. However, in the case of a hit made by the fencer who made the doubtful hit, the following will apply: *A subsequent hit must be scored if made by the fencer who made the doubtful hit without any hit having been made by the opponent.*

LEARNING EXPERIENCE

Fencer A attacks Fencer B, who parries and ripostes. Fencer A parries the riposte and counter-riposte. Judges 1 and 2 raise their arms. The referee halts the bout. Reviewing the action, the referee asks: "The original attack by Fencer A?" Judge 1 votes "Yes." Judge 2 votes "No." The referee votes "I abstain." The referee asks: "The riposte?" Judges 3 and 4 vote "No." The referee votes "I abstain." The referee then asks: "The counter-riposte by Fencer A?" Judges 1 and 2 vote "Yes." What is the decision? (Fencer B is hit.)

If there is doubt concerning the validity of the hit but not that there was a hit (that is, one "Yes" and one "Off target"), no other hit in this phrase can be scored.

LEARNING EXPERIENCE

Fencer A attacks Fencer B, who ripostes. Judges 1, 2, 3, and 4 raise their arms. The referee halts the bout. Reviewing the action, the referee asks: "The original attack by Fencer A?" Judge 1 votes "Yes." Judge 2 votes "Off target." The referee votes "I abstain." The referee then asks: "The riposte?" Judges 3 and 4 vote "Yes." What is the decision? (No score.)

The Timekeeper

The timekeeper notifies the referee when one minute of fencing time remains and terminates the bout at the end of that minute. The referee halts the bout, notifies the fencer of the one-minute warning, and states the score. At the end of that minute, the timekeeper, and no other official, terminates the bout.

The Scorekeeper

The scorekeeper is responsible for maintaining an accurate record of the scoring.

Individual tournament bouts are usually conducted by means of round-robin competition within pools consisting of four or more competitors. Frequently the number of entries requires several pools. Teammates (club, school, country, etc.) are separated, preventing them from competing against each other in the preliminary rounds

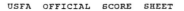

USFA OFFICIAL SCORE SHEET

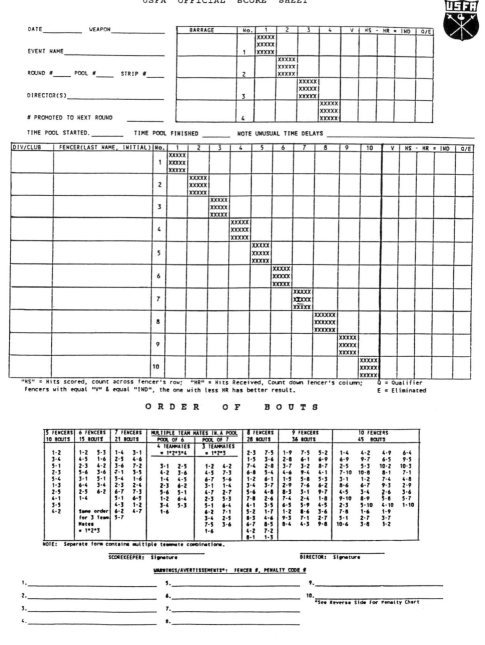

DATE_____ WEAPON_____

EVENT NAME_____

ROUND #_____ POOL #_____ STRIP #_____

DIRECTOR(S)_____

PROMOTED TO NEXT ROUND _____

TIME POOL STARTED._____ TIME POOL FINISHED _____ NOTE UNUSUAL TIME DELAYS _____

BARRAGE		No.	1	2	3	4	V	HS - HR = IND	Q/E
		1	XXXXX XXXXX XXXXX						
		2		XXXXX XXXXX XXXXX					
		3			XXXXX XXXXX XXXXX				
		4				XXXXX XXXXX XXXXX			

DIV/CLUB	FENCER(LAST NAME, INITIAL)	No.	1	2	3	4	5	6	7	8	9	10	V	HS - HR = IND	Q/E
		1	XXXXX XXXXX XXXXX											
		2		XXXXX XXXXX XXXXX										
		3			XXXXX XXXXX XXXXX									
		4				XXXXX XXXXX XXXXX								
		5					XXXXX XXXXX XXXXX							
		6						XXXXX XXXXX XXXXX						
		7							XXXXX XXXXX XXXXX					
		8								XXXXXX XXXXXX XXXXXX				
		9									XXXXX XXXXX XXXXX			
		10										XXXXX XXXXX XXXXX		

"HS" = Hits scored, count across fencer's row; "HR" = Hits Received, Count down fencer's column;   Q = Qualifier
Fencers with equal "V" & equal "IND", the one with less HR has better result.   E = Eliminated

ORDER OF BOUTS

5 FENCERS 10 BOUTS	6 FENCERS 15 BOUTS		7 FENCERS 21 BOUTS		MULTIPLE TEAM MATES IN A POOL				8 FENCERS 28 BOUTS				9 FENCERS 36 BOUTS				10 FENCERS 45 BOUTS			
					POOL OF 6		POOL OF 7													
					4 TEAMMATES = 1*2*3*4		3 TEAMMATES = 1*2*3													
1-2	1-2	5-3	1-4	3-1					2-3	7-5	1-9	7-5	5-2	1-4	4-2	4-9	6-4
3-4	4-5	1-6	2-5	4-6					1-5	3-6	2-8	6-1	6-9	6-9	9-7	6-5	9-5
5-1	2-3	4-2	3-6	7-2	3-1	2-5	1-2	4-2	7-4	2-8	3-7	3-2	8-7	2-5	5-3	10-2	10-3
2-3	5-6	3-6	7-1	3-5	4-2	3-6	4-5	7-3	6-8	5-4	4-6	9-4	4-1	7-10	10-8	8-1	7-1
5-4	3-1	5-1	5-4	1-6	1-4	4-5	6-7	5-6	1-2	6-1	1-5	5-8	5-3	3-1	1-2	7-4	4-8
1-3	6-4	3-4	2-3	2-4	2-3	6-2	3-1	1-4	3-4	3-7	2-9	7-6	6-2	8-6	6-7	9-3	2-9
2-5	2-5	6-2	6-7	7-3	5-6	5-1	4-7	2-7	5-6	4-8	8-3	3-1	9-7	4-5	3-4	2-6	3-6
4-1	1-4		5-1	6-5	1-2	6-4	2-3	5-3	7-8	2-6	7-4	2-4	1-8	9-10	8-9	5-8	5-7
3-5			4-3	1-2	3-4	5-3	5-1	6-4	4-1	3-5	6-5	5-9	4-5	2-3	5-10	4-10	1-10
4-2	Same order for 3 Team Mates = 1*2*3		6-2	4-7	1-6		6-2	7-1	5-2	1-7	1-2	8-6	3-6	7-8	1-6	1-9	
			5-7				3-4	2-5	8-3	4-6	9-3	7-1	2-7	5-1	2-7	3-7	
							7-5	3-6	6-7	8-5	8-4	4-3	9-8	10-6	3-8	3-2	
							1-6		4-2	7-2							
									8-1	1-3							

NOTE: Separate form contains multiple teammate combinations.

SCOREKEEPER: Signature _____   DIRECTOR: Signature _____

WARNINGS/AVERTISSEMENTS*: FENCER #, PENALTY CODE #

1._____ 5._____ 9._____
2._____ 6._____ 10._____
3._____ 7._____ *See Reverse Side for Penalty Chart
4._____ 8._____

USFA Official Score Sheet

wherever possible. In this case, the fencers scoring highest in each pool advance to the next round, when new pools are formed. This round-robin process continues until a final pool is attained.

Round-robin bouting in this final pool determines the winner. The number of qualifiers who can advance from one pool to the next is determined before the start of competition, and the order of bouting is governed by a fixed schedule prepared in advance.

Each fencer is represented by a number corresponding to the numbers in the vertical and horizontal columns on the score sheet. The order of bouts depends on the number of fencers in the pool (see the illustration, Order of Bouts). For example, in a pool of four competitors the first bout would be between Fencer A (number 1) and Fencer D (number 4).

The scorekeeper divides the score boxes in half horizontally and uses the lower part to record hits scored and the upper part to record victory (V) or defeat (number of hits scored). Total victories are recorded in the V (victory) column.

The standing or place of each fencer at the completion of a pool is determined by the number of victories. If two or more fencers who might normally qualify for the next round have an equal number of victories, their standing is determined by an indicator using the following formula: hits scored minus hits received.

For example, if Fencer A scored 15 hits and received 19, A's indicator would be -4. If Fencer B scored 16 hits and received 19, B's indicator would be -3. Fencer B would place higher than Fencer A. On the other hand, Fencer C, with 18 hits scored and 16 received, would have an indicator of $+2$ and would place higher than Fencer D, with 16 hits scored and 16 received, showing an indicator of 0. In the case of a tie with equal indicators, the fencer with the lowest number of hits received is placed highest. For a detailed table of indicators, consult the USFA rule book.

Should there be absolute equality of victories and indicators, the tied competitors fence a *barrage*. When, in the final pool, there is a tie for first place, the order is determined by a barrage.

In national competitions the format is as follows: There will be one round of pools. Some 80 percent of the competitors who enter the round of pools will be promoted to a direct elimination table.

Promotion from the pools and seeding into the direct elimination table will be determined by three indicators: (1) the number of victories divided by the number of bouts fenced (V/B); (2) the number of touches scored minus the number of touches received (TS − TR); (3) the fewer number of touches received. All promoted fencers will be placed in a direct elimination table with no change for teammate conflicts. There will be no *repêchage*. The direct elimination bouts are for 15 touches. When the 15th touch is awarded, regardless of time, the bout is over. The time of a direct elimination bout is divided into three rounds of 3 minutes each with a 1-minute break between rounds. There will be no bout to determine third place. The two fencers who lost in the bouts to qualify for the final bouts will both be awarded third place. In the bout for first place, if there is a tie at the end of the 9 minutes an additional minute will be fenced. If the tie is not broken during this additional minute, the victor is determined as in other direct elimination bouts.

By the 1994 National Championships, all fencers will be required to have their names printed on their uniforms.

Electrical Scoring and Officiating Responsibilities

With the introduction of electrical scoring machines, a somewhat different officiating technique is required because the electrical apparatus in most instances replaces the four judges.

The bout is directed by the referee, who moves up and down alongside the strip to follow the action while keeping the light signals in view. At the beginning of each bout, and whenever electrical weapons are changed, the referee must check the resistance of the spring in the point by means of a 500-gram weight for foil and 750-gram weight, as well as using shims to check the travel distance of the point for épée.

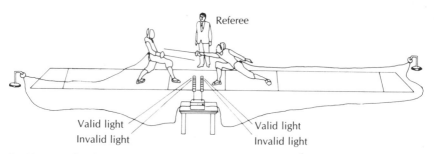

Referee

Valid light
Invalid light

Valid light
Invalid light

Positioning of Referee and Electrical Apparatus
(The invalid—off-target—light is used only in foil fencing.)

The point of the blade contains a spring attachment that, when depressed, breaks an electrical circuit and causes the apparatus to signal a hit. This hit activates a buzzer and a light. If the light is colored (red for one fencer, green for the other), the hit is valid. In foil fencing, if the light is white it indicates an invalid touch. However, the referee may declare a hit against a fencer who covers a valid target with an invalid one. An off-target hit in foil fencing (white light) halts the action and nullifies any subsequent action by either fencer until the bout is resumed.

For example, if both signal lights (white and colored) appear on the same side of the apparatus, an invalid hit has preceded a valid hit. The referee's decision in this instance is "no score." On the other hand, the electrical scoring device is so constructed that when a valid hit is followed by an off-target hit only the colored light goes on. It must also be noted that in foil and saber fencing the electrical apparatus does not indicate any priority in time between two or more hits that register at approximately the same time. It is the referee's function to award the touch by applying the principle of right-of-way, which gives the fencer who initiates an attack the right in an attempt to hit the target.

The fencer so threatened must defend or parry before riposting. The fencer who has parried acquires the right-of-way by resuming the attack. There are some exceptions to this rule. For example, when a compound attack is made and the opponent's stop-hit lands before the start of the final movement of the original attack, the counterattack has the right-of-way. Fencing tempo is not so much a time measure as an action measure. The referee employs the rule of right-of-way only when simultaneous or near-simultaneous hits are made. The speed and mobility of modern fencers create situations that may be difficult for novice officials to interpret, but this rule, when correctly interpreted, will help officials establish the orderly sequence of movements.

OFFICIATING DUTIES AND TECHNIQUES

A general knowledge of duties and specific techniques will help develop competency in officiating.

The referee is responsible for:

Making certain that the judges, scorekeeper, and timekeeper understand their duties and that the fencers understand the strip boundaries.

Visually checking all fencers approaching the strip, to be sure they are safely outfitted—for example, to detect such hazards as holes in the jacket, long hair draped over any part of the target area, and bare legs.

If electrical equipment is used, making arrangements for having the fencers hooked up so time is not lost.

Determining the sequence of movements by concentrating on the action of the blades, not the target. The target is the responsibility of the judges or the electrical apparatus.

Reconstructing only the phrase or portion of a phrase which directly affects the outcome, avoiding verbose reconstructions.

Speaking clearly and audibly, and stating decisions with certainty.

If an electrical machine is used, moving so that the machine is visible between the contestants at all times.

For the sake of clarity and uniformity, announcing "No score!" if no hit has been awarded, avoiding other wording, such as "Nothing done!"

Judges are responsible for:

Moving with the action on the strip.

When a hit is observed, valid or invalid, immediately and vigorously raising a hand high. Never hesitating.

Responding to the referee's question by reporting only what is seen, not what is heard.

Responding decisively and independently.

Avoiding intimidation by a fencer.

Scorekeepers are responsible for:

Announcing loudly and clearly: "(Name) and (Name) fencing. (Name) and (Name) on deck" before each bout. ("On deck" means that the two named opponents should be ready to fence next at the conclusion of the current bout.)

If the electrical scoring apparatus is not used, announcing the score clearly after each touch—for example, "3–2, for Mr. Jones."

When a pool of bouts has been completed, indicating on the score sheet the place each fencer earned, having the referee sign the sheet, then submitting it to the tournament chairperson.

Timekeepers are responsible for:

Timing only the interval between the referee's commands "Fence!" and "Halt!" unless otherwise instructed.

Calling the referee's attention as the last minute has begun. The referee will stop the bout and notify the competitors that one minute of fencing time remains.

Calling "Time!" loudly at the expiration of the final minute.

Those assigned to electrical machine operation are responsible for:

Making certain the apparatus faces the referee.

Waiting until the referee asks "Ready!" before clearing the machine.

Not clearing the machine prematurely.

Officiating in fencing requires special skills and provides a dynamic challenge for those who have the necessary attributes.

LEARNING EXPERIENCE

1. *Attend a fencing tournament in your locale. Carefully observe the referee. Mentally make your own decisions about the fencing action and compare your decision with that of the referee.*
2. *Volunteer to keep score or time at a fencing meet. Those in charge will gladly explain the proper procedures. Helping at a meet will familiarize you with tournament procedures and enable you to observe the fencing and the officiating.*
3. *Attend clinics, seminars, and workshops to improve your officiating skills.*

HIGHLIGHTS

1. List at least six skills and/or personal characteristics required of officials.
2. List the titles of the officials in a conventional bout and explain the duties of each.
3. Explain the difference between "Yes," "No," and "Abstain" by a judge and a referee.
4. Given any combination of the above votes by two judges and the referees, determine the correct decision.
5. Explain the rule of right-of-way and how it is employed in officiating.
6. Explain the proper use of a score-sheet.
7. Explain how the number of officials, responsibilities, and techniques used in an electrically scored bout differ from a conventional one.
8. Contact the USFA regarding their program for training and certifying referees.

8

Physical Fitness

Attaining a high fitness level requires a conditioning program designed for individual needs. Conditioning should be a progressive, continuing process in which the fencer engages several times a week throughout the year. It should not be limited to weekends or concentrated into one or two days. Regular medical checkups should be required, with particular emphasis on the individual's capacity to engage in strenuous physical activity (see Chapter 12 on Liability and Negligence). The instructor or coach should discuss the medical checkup reports with each fencer (or the parent/guardian of a minor as noted in Chapter 12) and should offer professional advice regarding potential problems, including excessive weakness or fatigue or abnormal body weight. Good general health habits are essential to conditioning.

Endurance, flexibility, speed and quickness, and agility are the fitness components necessary for achieving satisfaction and success in fencing. They can be developed with a program of exercises and drills. Naturally, the components are interrelated; improvement in any component will be accompanied by improvement in the others. Muscle efficiency will improve with conditioning. "Correct" movements require less energy, result in less fatigue, and are more efficient than movements considered incorrect.

The Learning Experiences that follow contain suggestions for developing certain fitness components related to specific body areas. They have proven their usefulness, but many others can be developed that relate directly to fencing skills. Individual differences, such as age and general health, require differing levels of intensity in the following as in any conditioning program. The level of intensity (dosage) recommended in these exercises reflects the level considered necessary for maintaining good physical condition after an adequate level has been achieved. Beginners should start at a lower level and increase the intensity or number of repetitions until they can perform at the recommended level. The instructor or coach should set the exercise dosage for each fencer as a recognition of the fencer's readiness for progressively higher competitive levels.

WARM-UP EXERCISES

Every workout or competition should begin with warm-up exercises designed to stretch the muscles and tendons and to prepare the body for more strenuous activity. The warm-ups should include the following:

Neck circumduction (5 to 10 repetitions).
Extended arm circling (20 to 30 repetitions).
Torso twisting (5 to 10 repetitions).
Side bending (5 to 10 repetitions).
Opposite-toe touching (10 to 15 repetitions).
Half knee bends (5 to 10 repetitions).
Sitting hamstring stretcher (3 to 5 repetitions).
Achilles stretcher (3 to 5 repetitions).

LEARNING EXPERIENCE—WARM-UPS

Experiment to discover the point at which a warm-up has loosened your muscles without exhausting you. Feeling "loose" and beginning to perspire are generally signs that you are sufficiently warmed up.

ENDURANCE

Muscular and cardiorespiratory endurance is necessary for extended competitions. Even a small number of bouts requires endurance if the fencing phrases are lengthy.

Developing endurance and strength requires application of the "overload principle," which challenges the body a little more at each session. Initially muscles will ache, but the pain will disappear as muscle tone and endurance develop. Merely repeating easy workloads will not build endurance.

Endurance also helps improve the psychological factors of motivation and the will to endure pain and discomfort. In personality development this will is called persistence. No amount of discussion will develop this trait; its origin is mental but its attainment is physical. A person must want to fence!

LEARNING EXPERIENCE—ENDURANCE

1. Jog-walk-jog. *The fencer should check with a physician to determine the recommended maximum heartbeat level for use in monitoring his or her development with this exercise. Then each fencer should establish a jog-walk-jog schedule for optimal benefit.*

     Purpose: *To improve cardiorespiratory fitness.*

     Dosage: *Thirty minutes a session, at least four sessions a week.*

     Variations: *Increase the distance (or time) for each jog until a minimum of two miles can be covered. Alternatives are bench stepping, cycling, rope skipping, distance swimming, and specially designed exercises.*

2. Running continuously. *A more intense training exercise than the jog-walk-jog, provided the activity can be sustained for longer than 10 minutes.*

     Purpose: *To promote cardiorespiratory fitness.*

     Dosage: *11 to 12 minutes a session, at least 3 sessions a week.*

     Variations: *Distance cycling, rope skipping, distance swimming.*

FLEXIBILITY

With good flexibility, the muscle can move efficiently throughout its range, allowing optimal performance with relatively little chance of injury. Flexibility is governed by individual bone structure and soft tissue; bone structure is essentially fixed, whereas soft tissue can be stretched.

More-flexible thigh muscles permit a longer lunge, and a greater reach is possible with more-flexible arm and shoulder muscles. Well-toned and flexible muscles do not clutch, grab, or feel tight. Stretching exercises should be performed slowly. Progress should be gradual. Avoid sudden, jerky movements that might strain muscles or tendons.

LEARNING EXPERIENCE—FLEXIBILITY

1. Static stretch. *Move each body or limb segment individually through its range of movement until a "pain threshold" is reached, then maintain this stretched posi-*

tion for three seconds. Remember that stretching should be performed slowly, without jerks or bounces that can cause injury. This exercise is best performed along with the daily warm-up exercises.

2. Trunk flexion. Sit with legs fully extended and feet together against a bench or board. Extend the arms and slowly stretch forward (as far beyond the board as possible), then hold this position for a count of three. Measure the distance between the tips of the fingers and the board—either short of the board or beyond it. Measures beyond the board are plus scores; those short of it are minus scores. Effort should be made to increase the extent of the stretch gradually.

    Purpose: To increase trunk flexion and to stretch the back muscles and back thigh muscles (hamstrings).
    Dosage: 5 to 10 repetitions.
    Variations: Toe touching, trunk twisting, side stretching.

3. Trunk extension. Lie prone (face down) on the floor. A partner should straddle your legs, holding them and buttocks down. Place both hands behind your neck and raise the chest and head off the floor as far as possible. Hold this position for a count of three. Measure the distance from chin to floor.

    Purpose: To increase the range of backward upper body movement.
    Dosage: 5 to 10 repetitions.
    Variations: Toe touching, trunk twisting, side stretching, butterfly swimming stroke.

4. Shoulder lift. Lie prone (face down) on the floor. Extend the arms, holding a bar or wand in both hands (palms down) with chin on the floor. Lift the wand and chin as high as possible and hold for a count of three. Measure the distance from shoulder to floor.

    Purpose: To increase the range of movement of the shoulder girdle and back.
    Dosage: 5 to 10 repetitions.
    Variations: Arm circling, toe touching, trunk twisting, side stretching, shoulder shrugs with weights, shoulder rolls hanging from a bar.

5. Lunge stretcher. Assume a well-balanced lunge position. Place the left hand on the left hip and the right hand on the right knee. Push against the hip, forcing the thigh to stretch as the hip is lowered and the lunge elongates. Maintain this position for 12 seconds. Reverse the leg positions and repeat.

    Purpose: To stretch the thigh muscles and increase the range of movement.
    Dosage: 5 to 10 repetitions.
    Variation: Stride stretcher. With knees on the floor, place one foot forward so the knee is directly over the heel of the foot. Press the hips downward and forward while keeping both knees stationary. Hold for 30 seconds. This exercise is good for lower back and hip flexibility.

STRENGTH

Strength in the hands and shoulders is necessary for holding and manipulating the weapon throughout the bout. The legs must be strong for maintaining body balance, maintaining the fencing stance for long periods, and generating power for driving the body forward quickly with great force.

Current research indicates that an increase in muscle-fiber size is a factor in developing strength. The overload principle appears to be most useful in a strength-developing exercise program.

LEARNING EXPERIENCE—STRENGTH

1. Ball squeeze. *Practice squeezing a tennis ball with each hand.*
    Purpose: *To increase the strength of the fingers, hand, and forearm.*
    Dosage: *20 to 30 repetitions with each hand.*
    Variations: *Substitute balls with more resistance.*
Use steel coil-spring exercisers for the same purpose. Periodically check the grip strength with a Stoelting Grip Dynamometer.

2. Push-ups. *Assume a prone position (face down) with the palms at the shoulder point. Push with the arms fully extended while keeping the body and legs straight. Flex the arms and lower the chest to the floor. Repeat.*
    Purpose: *To increase the strength and endurance of the arm extensors, the shoulder girdle, and the chest muscles.*
    Dosage: *25 to 30 repetitions.*
    Variations: *Pull-ups (with palms outward); dips on parallel bars.*
3. Four-count leg exercises. *Lie supine (on the back) with hands at your sides. Raise legs slowly about 18 inches (45 centimeters). Hold for at least one second. Spread legs wide and then return. Hold for one second, lower legs gently to the floor. Repeat with a slow count.*
    Purpose: *To increase the strength and endurance of the thighs and abdominal muscles.*
    Dosage: *10 to 20 repetitions.*
    Variations: *Bent-knee situps, flutter kicks, sitting tucks.*
4. Wall sit. *Assume a sitting position with the back against a wall and the knees together. The upper legs should be parallel with the floor and the lower legs should form a right angle at the knee. The buttocks should be knee-high. Hold this position.*
    Purpose: *To increase the strength and endurance of the calves and thighs.*
    Dosage: *20 seconds to 1 minute for each repetition. Five or more repetitions.*
    Variations: *Endurance hops, bench stepping, toe risers with weights.*
5. Sit and stand. *Sit back-to-back on the floor with a partner, legs flexed and arms locked. On command, rise together by pressing backs and extending legs. On command, reverse the procedure and return to the sitting position.*
    Purpose: *To increase the strength and endurance of the calves and the thighs.*
    Dosage: *5 to 10 repetitions.*
    Variations: *Vary the quickness of commands and execution. Endurance hops, bench stepping, half knee bends with weights.*
6. Wrist rotation with weights. *With a 5-pound weight in each hand, palms down, extend the arms forward parallel to the floor. Slowly rotate the wrists clockwise*

for 10 repetitions, then repeat counterclockwise. Increase the weights as strength develops.

    Purpose: *To increase the strength and endurance of wrists, arms, and shoulders.*

    Dosage: *10 to 20 repetitions.*

    Variations: *Repeat above with palms facing upward; flex the wrists up and down with weights.*

7.   Wrist roller with weights. *This apparatus is a bar with a rope or cord at the center, by which a weight may be suspended. Start with a 5-pound weight suspended from the bar and reaching the floor from the shoulder height. Support this with arms extended. Rotate the bar forward to lift the weight, using the hands alternately and winding the rope onto the bar. Reverse the wrist action, slowly lowering the weight to the floor.*

    Purpose: *To increase the strength and endurance of the wrists, arms, and shoulders.*

    Dosage: *Start with 5 repetitions and gradually increase to 20.*

    Variations: *Increase the weight as strength develops. Perform the same exercise with the elbows pressed against the sides.*

SPEED AND QUICKNESS

Speed and quickness play a vital part in achieving success in fencing. Both overall tempo and reaction time are involved.

Increased strength and flexibility improve speed. Learning and applying correct skills improves both speed and quickness, as improper or unnecessary movements are eliminated. Warming up the muscles helps them work more smoothly and quickly.

LEARNING EXPERIENCE—SPEED AND QUICKNESS

1.   Squat thrusts. *From a standing position, move to a squat position by bending both knees, and place hands on the floor about shoulder width apart. With the arms extended, thrust the legs back so the body is straight. Return to the squat position, then return to the standing position. Increase the tempo as ability improves.*

    Purpose: *To strengthen the muscles of the arms, legs, and body.*

    Dosage: *15 to 30 repetitions.*

    Variations: *Alternate striding from the front-leaning rest position, rope skipping, wind sprints.*

2.   Drumming. *In the on-guard position, on the balls of the feet, alternately lift each foot from the floor rapidly (similar to running in place). Continue for 20 seconds, rest 10 seconds, then repeat 5 times. Speed should be increased as much as possible while maintaining balance in the on-guard position.*

Purpose: *To increase the speed of foot and leg movements.*
Dosage: *5 to 10 sets.*
Variations: *Advance and retreat while drumming.*

3.   Pin-the-glove. *The fencer assumes the on-guard position at lunge distance from a wall. A partner releases a glove held against a wall at 2.5 meters height. The fencer must lunge and pin the glove against the wall before it reaches the floor. As the fencer's skills improve, the glove should be dropped from lower points.*
Purpose: *To sharpen reaction time and develop quickness.*
Dosage: *15 to 30 repetitions.*
Variation: *The glove can be thrown on the wall from a point behind the fencer.*

AGILITY

Fencers must move speedily and react quickly, and also constantly change direction without losing balance. They must be light and bouncy on their feet and able to maneuver their bodies like dancers.

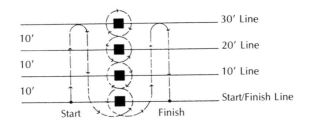

LEARNING EXPERIENCE—AGILITY

1.   Thirty-foot agility run. *Station four obstacles, such as chairs, 10 feet apart, with one placed at the start-finish line. Start from a prone position near the start point. On the command "Go," run directly to the 30-foot line and return by the same route to the start line. Continue to run, zigzagging around the obstacles to and from the 30-foot line. Then, upon reaching the start line, sprint to the 30-foot line and return to the finish-start line.*
Purpose: *To gain facility in changing direction without losing balance.*
Dosage: *Until course can be run successfully at a reasonable speed.*
Variations: *Advancing or retreating in response to signals by the coach/ instructor (whistles, hand claps, or gestures). Following a leader through the course while keeping a specified distance.*

2.   Burpee (squat thrust) four-count exercise. *Start by standing in the basic position. On the count of one, assume the squat position and place the hands on the*

ground. On the count of two, extend both legs to the rear. On the count of three, return to the squat position. On the count of four, resume the original basic position.

Purpose: *To gain facility in changing positions from the motionless state.*

Dosage: *15 to 30 seconds continuously, then repeat until the exercise can be done without loss of balance.*

Variations: *Competitive games—dodge ball, spud, bombardment dodge ball (using several balls). Competitive relays—sprint baton relay, leapfrog relay, rope-skip relay.*

HIGHLIGHTS

1. List and define the components of fitness required for optimal fencing performance.
2. Define the overload principle and tell what effect it has on fitness.
3. Explain the effect that health habits have on fencing performance.
4. Explain the relationship between warm-up and performance.
5. Maintain a personal schedule, in which you record conditioning activities and dosage and note changes in your fitness level.
6. Correlate fencing performances with fitness levels at various times during the year.

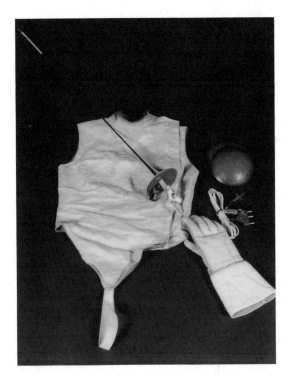

9

Maintenance of Electrical Equipment

EQUIPMENT FOR COMPETITION

Competition fencing requires supplementary equipment. Choice of personal equipment will become more selective as the fencer improves. The individual's choices usually include the weight and balance of the weapon, the weight and fit of the uniform, the weight and design of the mask, and the proper fit and traction of the shoes.

The official uniform includes the full jacket, knickers, shoes, socks, and glove. A white uniform is required for competition. Colored knee socks may be worn for institutional identification.

When selecting a uniform, consider the quality and type of material (gabardine, duck, stretch, or twill), comfort and ease of movement, and style. For long tournaments, or if the fencer perspires profusely, a second jacket is advisable.

Full Jacket. The jacket usually has a double lining in the sleeve, under the armpits, and across the chest. The rules require that women's jackets carry additional padding across the chest, a protective bra, and a padded vest worn under the jacket. All fencers are required to wear, under the jacket, a one-sleeved plastron for the weapon arm. It is held in place by elastic or buttoned straps and is usually made of gabardine, twill, cotton, or synthetic material.

For international competitions, underarm protectors and undershorts made of Kavlar material are required. Arm patches, if used, are worn only on the sleeve of the rear arm.

Knickers. Fencing knickers are required to be worn in competitions. Knee-length socks are necessary for leg protection. Adhesive tape may be used to prevent the socks from sliding down and exposing the legs.

Warm-Up Trousers and Jackets. Warm-up clothing is available in a wide variety of styles, fabrics, and colors. It is worn to retain body heat and to prevent chilling between bouts. All Olympic teams, most school teams, and many individuals wear warm-up clothes.

Shoes. Fencing shoes should have reinforced areas to prevent wear and have treads designed for good traction. Although more expensive, they usually wear longer than regular tennis or gym shoes. Fencers subject to heel bruises may choose to wear a plastic heel cup inside the shoe of the leading foot.

Socks. Socks are available in a variety of fabrics (cotton, wool, nylon, and other) and should cover the forelegs. The choice of fabric and style is left to the fencer.

Gloves. Fencing gloves should have a cuff or gauntlet that overlaps the sleeve of the jacket. Gloves designed for electrical fencing have a hole through which the body cord emerges.

ELECTRICAL FENCING EQUIPMENT

Electrical fencing requires each combatant to have an electric weapon, a body cord, and a metallic vest.

Electrical Weapon. The electrical weapon is heavier than the conventional one for training. Most beginners use a French handle to hold the foil or épée, but if there is difficulty controlling the electrical weapon, it might be advisable to try an orthopedic handle.

Tournament regulations require each fencer to have two operable weapons because mechanical failures sometimes occur during bouts. If it is necessary to borrow equipment, the fencer must assume responsibility for any damage to it.

Body Cord. Great care should be exercised in handling the body cord, especially when it is being connected to the reel or being disconnected from it. During storage or transportation, it should not be bent at sharp angles or pinched by tight packing against hard objects.

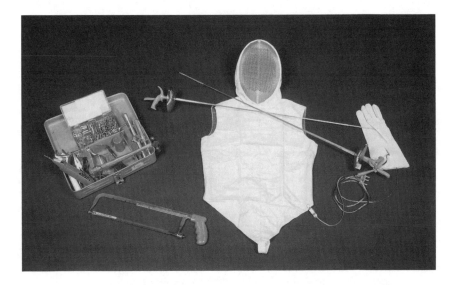

Metallic Vest. The metallic vest worn over the valid target area is made of lamé fabric, which has metallic threads woven into it. Under this, a vinyl lining acts as a buffer between the metallic fabric and the inevitably perspiration-dampened jacket. Perspiration, frequent hits in an area, and repeated folding can rupture the metallic threads. There is no magic formula to prevent corrosion, holes, or broken wires. However, the metallic garments will last a long time with proper care and attention. It is recommended that they be carried on a hanger in a ventilated plastic bag and aired and dried after every competition.

Holes, tears, or dead (nonconducting) spots can be repaired with fresh lamé patches or swatches. The electrical jacket should be washed in lukewarm water with mild soap or detergent and hung to dry. Do not wring out the garments. All fencing garments should be drip-dried.

Mask. The fencing mask must be made of strong mesh, rustproofed by hot tinning. The wires must have a minimum diameter of 1 millimeter before being tinned and should be spaced no more than 2.1 millimeters apart. For foil, the mesh must be insulated inside and out.

Masks come in three sizes—small, medium, and large—and are adjusted to fit by changing the shape of the back spring (head support). The bib and trim must be white.

Tools. Several basic tools are required to maintain equipment. A small pouch or bag can be used for such tools as a screwdriver, pliers, a test weight, a small signal tester or ohmmeter, shims, a small portable vise, an Allen wrench, a jeweler's screwdriver, emery paper, electrician's or plastic tape, extra retaining screws, and springs.

All participants in fencing should learn to diagnose troubles in electrical equipment and to repair them, because the working order of personal equipment is the responsibility of each fencer. The referee can annul only the last hit made before an equipment fault has been established. Therefore, each fencer has the responsibility to watch for any erratic equipment performance and report it immediately. For most problems, a procedure that will locate the faulty component in a logical and progressive manner can be established.

Weapon Bag. A weapon bag is a practical necessity for carrying fencing equipment. Bags of canvas, vinyl, or leather are available in various sizes to satisfy both individual and team needs. It is recommended that clothing, shoes, and gloves be packed in individual plastic bags to prevent moisture from affecting the equipment. Bags should be brushed and aired frequently, especially after a heavy workout or a tournament.

LEARNING EXPERIENCE—SUPPLEMENTARY EQUIPMENT

1. *Compare the comfort, wearing quality, and washability of fencing uniform materials (gabardine, duck, stretch, twill). Which do you prefer and why?*
2. *Practice replacing a spring in the tip of the blade, taping the blade, and replacing the blade.*

HIGHLIGHTS

1. List the components of an official fencing uniform.
2. List the items required for electrical fencing.
3. Explain the advantages of using an electric foil or épée with an orthopedic handle.
4. Describe how you would care for and maintain your personal gear, including electrical equipment.

MAINTAINING ELECTRICAL EQUIPMENT

The fencer must have a thorough understanding of the electrical weapon and equipment and the procedure for ensuring proper performance.

Electrical Scoring Equipment

Officiating and scoring became more efficient and objective with the introduction of electrical foil weapons and recording devices during the 1955 World Championships.* The modern recording apparatus has made it possible to serve

*The electrical épée had been introduced much earlier, about 1936.

all three weapons: foil, épée, and saber. In official tournaments the equipment inludes:

A recording machine (scoring apparatus).
Extension lights.
Two reels.
Two floor cables connecting the reels to the recording (scoring) machine.
An extension cord to electrical outlet.
A metallic strip (piste), grounded or neutralized by a cable attachment to a reel or to the recording machine in order to prevent touches on the strip (piste) from being recorded.

The scoring apparatus for épée fencing requires only two lights (either red or green) to register touches against either or both fencers. Only in épée fencing can double hits be scored. The scoring apparatus for foil fencing requires four lights—two (one white and one colored) representing each fencer. The white lights indicate off-target or invalid touches, while the colored lights represent valid-target touches. If both colored lights go on, the decision rests with the referee of the bout in accordance with foil conventions and the rule of right-of-way.

It is necessary to remember that there is no "off target" in saber fencing. The white light in saber indicates that somewhere in the electric chain there is improper contact.

Electrical Equipment for
Competition

Electrical Fencing Equipment

The fencer's metallic vest is designed to cover only the valid target area and is worn over the fencing jacket. The insulated body cord is worn inside the sleeve of the weapon arm and extends down the back beneath the jacket. One end of the cord is connected to the electrical weapon socket located inside the foil guard, the other end of the body cord is connected to a wire mounted in a spring-loaded reel. The clip on the body cord is then attached to the metallic vest.

The Electrical Foil

The foil is designed electrically as a continuous circuit. It employs a "break" circuit—that is, the point, when depressed, opens a normally closed guard socket, runs along the groove in the blade, enters the point base, and ends by resting solidly against the point pressure spring in a small insulated cup. The circuit is continued through this spring to the insulated core of the point. It extends to the point base and back through the blade to the socket inside the bell guard. When at rest, the point is held forward by the spring. A touch (tip of the foil touching an opponent with a minimum force of 500 grams) pushes the point back on the spring, "breaking" the circuit. The bell guard is neutralized (or grounded) by means of wiring inside the socket so that a touch on the guard will not register.

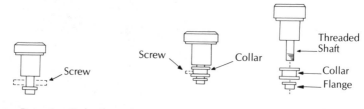

Flange-Retention Style   Collar Style

Checking Electrical Weapons

Electrical weapons should be checked before each competition.

Blades. Check for rust, dust, and dirt. Emery cloth or fine sandpaper can remove rust and the like. Be careful not to damage wires. For foil blades only, tape the front 15 centimeters (about 6 inches) of blade, starting just behind the retaining screws. Tape the foil tip with one-inch black electrician's tape. Check the spare blades too. They should fit handles with the same length of tang and have the same depth of threading.

Check the resistance of the electrical circuit. It should not exceed 3.5 ohms with the point at rest. With the point depressed, the reading should not exceed 500 ohms. Resistance from any point on the blade and guard to the ground connector of the socket must not exceed 2 ohms.

Tips. Check the tip-retaining screws and replace any that are loose or worn. Check the springs and replace them if necessary. To pass inspection, the foil spring must be strong enough to push up a 500-gram weight (for the épée spring, a 750-gram weight).

Inspect the tip for looseness. Tighten with pliers slowly and carefully. Avoid crunching the cylinder housing or stripping the wire insulation.

Guards. Check the diameter of the bell guard (see the USFA rule book for the exact dimensions). Inspect the guard for rust or other stains. Remove them with emery cloth or fine sandpaper. Check the socket inside the guard. There should be no loose nuts, screws, or bare wire showing.

Inspect the wire-insulating sleeve. The wire (two wires for épée) must be completely covered by one piece of insulating sleeving from the point where the wire enters the guard to where it is fastened to the socket for the body wire. Check the condition of the thumb pad. Every electrical weapon requires a thumb pad to protect the wires from the fingers.

Handles. Check to be sure the handle is properly notched. The notch (half-circle) should allow space for the blade wire in its sleeve to pass through without being pinched. Check the handle insulation. All handles must be insulated. Those not commercially insulated must be covered with insulating tape.

Pommels. Check the pommel fastening. It must be secure. Loose pommels may raise the electrical resistance and cause off-target signals. Remember, the saber pommel must be completely insulated. All foil-épée pommels for French-handle weapons should be electrically insulated.

Checking Electrical Gear

Body Cords. For the continental type, check the tightness of the two set screws and the plug springs. Tighten the plug springs by splaying if necessary. For the twist-lock cord, check to be sure the central screw is tight. Check all soldered joints. Repair them if they are not secure.

Check the crocodile clips for proper functioning (Mueller No. 27s are recommended). If the clip is defective or the spring is too weak, it must be replaced. Article 217 of the USFA rule book specifies that the crocodile clip is to be attached "to the back of the metallic jacket on the side of the weapon arm." Check the crocodile wire length. It should not be less than 40 centimeters.

Check the resistance at both ends of the body cord. Resistance at either end should not exceed 0.5 ohm.

Metallic Jackets (Lamés). Check the jacket for proper fit. It should completely cover the fencer's valid target area. Inspect the insulating material. If there are any tears or cracks, they must be repaired with insulating tape or replaced.

Thoroughly inspect the metallic threads in the lamé. Pay particular attention to major perspiration areas, such as those around the neck and under the armpits. The electrical resistance between any two points on the surface of the lamé may not exceed 5 ohms. Any holes, tears, or dead spots can be repaired with lamé patches or swatches. The electrical resistance should be thoroughly checked after patching.

Foil Mask. Inspect the insulating material. Small tears or cracks may be repaired with insulating tape. If the insulation is damaged extensively, the mask must be either replaced or refurbished.

Any Mask. Check the trim on the mask to be sure it is securely fastened to the mask and that there are no tears or breaks. If necessary, it can be repaired with tape.

Inspect the bib for cracks, tears, or incomplete attachment to the mask. The bib must be attached to the mask so that the weapon cannot penetrate between the mask and the bib. Safety demands that the bib be replaced if torn or cracked. A bib should be clean and free from any defects. Rules require the bib to be white.

Check the wire mesh. Be sure the wires are the proper size and spaced correctly (see Chapter 9). Check to be certain the mesh will withstand the 12 kilogram punch test. If the mesh is damaged or fails the punch test it must be replaced.

A second check should be made at the competition site, just before the competition.

Foils and Body Cords. Use two- or three-weapon electrical scoring machines without floor cables and reels. Set the switch to foil. Hook up two foils to two body cords and plug the cords into the machine. Connect the machine to an electrical outlet and switch the machine to "On." The pilot light should go on. If any other light goes on, press the reset button. If the machine resets, all is fine. If not, change weapons and/or body cords until the machine resets.

Press the foil points against each guard. No lights should go on. Check for off-target hits by depressing the foil tips singly and together. Use the reset button between touches. Only the white lights should register.

Test for valid hits by pressing the foil tips on the alligator clip of the opposite body cord. A valid touch signal (colored light) should register. Test both sides.

TESTING SCORING MACHINES

Machines with Floor Cables and Reels. If the machine is functioning properly, the tests should be repeated with the reels and the floor cables.

Machines with a Metallic Strip. If a metallic strip (piste) is being used, depress the foil tip on the piste. If it is properly grounded, no score will register.

A thorough and systematic check should be made at the end of the season. Perform a complete check, repair, and storage routine:

Take inventory of all equipment.
Make all necessary repairs.
Thoroughly clean all equipment.
Prepare for storage using a light application of suitable machine oil.
Store equipment in a well-ventilated area.

Taking care of scoring machines will prevent expensive malfunctions and repairs.

Up to this point nothing has been said about scoring-machine malfunctions. This postponement has been intentional. Of all possible troubles, those originating with the scoring machine are by far the least frequent, and in trouble-shooting it is best to play the percentages. This is not to say that the machines may not have eccentricities. They do, but for the most part the malfunctions are easily identifiable.

All machines, transistorized or not, can overheat, with characteristics that might vary from one machine to the next. Illumination of the lights for no apparent reason is one such characteristic. The light may become either dim or bright. In either case, disconnecting the machine from its power source when not in use will usually control the situation.

Electromechanical relays may get dirty after several seasons of use or incorrect storage. If this happens, resetting can become almost impossible and it will be necessary to have the relays cleaned, preferably by a professional.

Machine repair is relatively expensive because it requires the services of a professional. Because of this expense, the following points are very important:

The decision that a machine malfunction exists should be based on a detailed, careful check (such as that outlined above) to be sure an expense is not incurred unnecessarily.

When the malfunction is identified, its characteristics should be noted as thoroughly as possible. In this way, the time required for a professional to service the machine can be kept to the minimum.

LEARNING EXPERIENCE—ELECTRIC FOIL PROCEDURES FOR CHECKING EQUIPMENT

1. *Compare different scoring equipment. Which do you prefer and why?*
2. *Compare the continental type (two-prong) and the twist-lock type of body cords. Which do you prefer and why?*
3. *Ask an armorer or a knowledgeable fencer to explain and demonstrate the operation of the electrical fencing apparatus.*

HIGHLIGHTS

1. List the equipment required to host an official competition.
2. Describe the electrical circuit in foil fencing.
3. Practice repairing any holes, tears, or dead spots on a metallic vest with a lamé patch or swatch. Check the electrical resistance of the vest after patching it.

10

Conducting Tournaments

Fencers should learn to help organize and conduct fencing tournaments. Organizing a tournament can be fun, but it does require careful planning. Tournaments differ in size and importance and therefore will not all require the same degree of effort. However, every tournament does demand attention to detail. In addition to proper planning, the smooth conduct of a tournament depends on the full cooperation of organizers, officials, coaches, and competitors. Understanding the problems of organizing and conducting tournaments not only enables the fencer to assist when called upon, but also develops a keen appreciation for the need to adhere to rules and regulations.

MASTER PLAN AND SCHEDULING

Two to Twelve Months in Advance. Plan early. Decide on the purpose and type of tournament. List things to be done so that an action plan may be drawn up.

Clear dates for use of the tournament site; check school and institution calendars to avoid conflicts. Arrange for referees and possible alternates. Draw up a budget.

Order awards. Arrange for public information and publicity. Arrange for necessary equipment so that availability will be guaranteed. Organize committees.

One Month to Six Weeks in Advance. Organize the tournament and assign duties accompanied by job descriptions. List equipment and materials needed. Arrange for locker, meal, and refreshment facilities. Arrange for overnight accommodations, parking areas, and medical personnel and equipment. Secure scorekeepers, timers, and all other necessary personnel. Draw up a layout for the competition area, including strip locations.

One Day to Two Weeks in Advance. Organize the pools for the tournament immediately after all entries are in. Have programs printed and ready for distribution.

The Day Before the Tournament. Set up the registration desk. Review all assignments with personnel. Prepare all facilities and equipment.

The Day of the Tournament. Start early to recheck the list of things to do. Welcome the participants. Start on time. Be constantly alert to any potential problems during the tournament so they can be dealt with expeditiously.

Inform news media of the tournament results. Be certain the competition area is cleaned. Check, return, and secure equipment.

The Day After the Tournament. Evaluate the tournament in writing and file materials that might be of assistance for future tournaments. Write "thank you" notes to all helpful persons and organizations. Send results and photographs to *American Fencing, The Swordmaster,* or other appropriate publications.

For more detailed information on conducting tournaments, consult the USFA rule book or contact the USFCA (U.S. Fencing Coaches Association). A complete discussion of organizing tournaments is contained in *Tournament Guide for the National Collegiate Championships,* 3rd edition (1980), by M. R. Garret, Candice Corcoran, and Kathleen Russell.

ENTRY INFORMATION

Entry blanks and accompanying material should provide all the information a participant needs, including the purpose, type, and eligibility requirements of the tournament; the location, date, sponsor; awards; dressing facilities; the entry fee; and the entry deadline. Travel, overnight lodging, eating accommodations, and ticket information should be included where applicable.

PERSONNEL REQUIREMENTS

Small Tournaments

The size of the tournament will determine the division of duties and the number of persons required. Small tournaments (twenty-four or fewer entrants) would require the following personnel:

Tournament chairman. Determines pools and prepares bout sheets; checks strips, equipment, and supplies; assigns referees, timers, and scorekeepers and lists their duties; makes introductions, announcements, and presents awards.

Scorekeepers and timers. See Chapter 7.

Referees. Review general rules and groundrules with the fencers; check safety of the equipment and the uniforms; review judging (if judges are used) and directing techniques.

Bout committee. Acts as a court of appeals and a resource for interpretation of rules.

Equipment tester. Tests and validates electrical weapons, body cords, masks, sensors, and metallic garments.

Large Tournaments

Large tournaments require appropriately larger numbers of the same personnel that small tournaments require. In addition, the chairman of the large tournament should consider appointing people to act in the following capacities:

Head scorekeeper. Records scoring information for each fencer on a master scoring chart as well as on the individual scorecards; assigns a scorekeeper for each strip; appoints a captain to assign timers and scorers to the strips for each round and to distribute and collect the scorecards and supplies.

Fencing-area manager. Supervises all arrangements in the fencing area, such as placement of mats, tables, and chairs; takes inventory of equipment (including loaned equipment); supervises a crew for dismantling and storing equipment; takes responsibility for cleaning up the area.

Armorer. Available for repairing electrical equipment.

COMPETITION AREA

The safety of contestants, officials, and spectators is of primary importance in arranging space. Equipment such as metallic strips and scoring apparatus should be set up properly before the tournament. Poor organization of the competition area represents a hazard to all concerned and could become an important factor in a potential liability suit.

The minimum floor area designated for each strip should be 17 meters by 5.5 meters (about 56 feet by 18 feet). The area manager should prepare a scaled plan of the area, marking off areas required for fencing strips, scoring tables, publicity personnel, spectators, and other needs. If the building does not provide suitable separation of spectators and contestants, an area must be set aside for spectators. This should be separated from the contestants by a physical barrier (e.g., a rope) at a suitable distance from any bouting.

REGULATION STRIPS

Strips are normally about 6 feet (1.8 meters) wide and 56 to 59 feet (17 to 18 meters) long to allow for at least a 5-foot (about 1.5 meters) safety zone at each end. Markings on the strips should be in accordance with the USFA rules. If strips are not available, masking tape (or other suitable tape) is acceptable for outlining the strips. If the floor tends to be slippery, precautionary measures should be taken to eliminate the potential for injury.

Every strip (whether rubber or metallic) must be secured to provide firm footing. The sides and ends should be taped to the floor with carpet tape or other strong tape at least 4 inches wide. Be sure the strips are securely taped to the floor.

ELECTRICAL SCORING APPARATUS

Be sure that spare machines and spare reels are available. A table for scorekeepers, timekeepers, and scoring apparatus should be provided for each strip. Also needed are clipboards, pencils, time clocks, scoresheets, and chairs. Test weights, shims for épée, and sensors for saber will be needed if electrical weapons are to be used.

SPECIAL SITE ARRANGEMENTS

Certain special arrangements at the site can be of great help in the smooth conduct of a tournament. These include a designated parking area, a reporting or registration desk, a practice area, a dressing area, lockers, a lounge area, a refreshment area, storage space, a first-aid area, and seating for the spectators. Tournaments can often benefit from music or some form of entertainment during competition breaks.

CLOSING CEREMONY

Even though awards are not the primary reason for holding a tournament, they can and should be symbolic of achievement. The awards can be purchased, but members of the arts departments of colleges or universities could be called upon to design them.

The ceremony should be dignified and colorful. Inviting a well-known person or school official to make the presentations may enhance the ceremony.

LEARNING EXPERIENCE—ORGANIZING TOURNAMENTS

1. Volunteer your help in organizing and conducting a fencing tournament.
2. Write an article for the local newspaper (or magazine) about a tournament in which you have worked or fenced.
3. Evaluate a fencing tournament. Use the following categories as guides: preliminary planning, safety considerations, accommodations for teams, publicity, competition area, personnel, equipment, ceremony, follow-up.

HIGHLIGHTS

1. List the personnel needed to conduct an interclass tournament.
2. What safety factors should the tournament organizer keep in mind?
3. Draw up an appropriate entry-blank form.
4. What information (other than that on the entry form) should a potential entrant receive?
5. Design the competition-area layout for five fencing strips and the necessary related equipment, using basketball-court dimensions (typically 50 feet by 94 feet).
6. What considerations should organizers take into account for convenience and comfort?

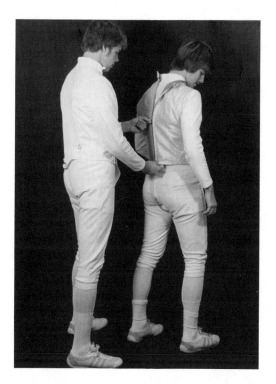

11

Safety

Safety must be a concern of all persons engaged in fencing—participants, instructors, coaches, officials, supervisors, and equipment manufacturers. The goals of this chapter and the next are:

To increase everyone's alertness to fencing safety.
To point out everyone's responsibility for fencing safety.
To describe safety measures and precautions.
To discuss liability and negligence.

THE COST OF ACCIDENTS AND INJURIES

According to most definitions, an accident is an unplanned event. An accident might happen to anyone, given certain conditions and/or acts. The undesirable results of an accident in fencing—besides probable injury—may be anger, frustration, and embarrassment for the injured party, plus money costs for medical care and time lost from fencing and other activities.

In most instances, medical care for athletes (which may include the services of athletic trainers and use of training supplies and equipment) and the insurance overhead become a cost to the sponsoring institution.

RESPONSIBILITY FOR SAFETY MEASURES

Although medical and insurance expenses are measured in dollars and cents, the fencing instructor or coach is concerned above all with the athlete's well-being. Proper safety measures practiced by the instructor or coach and the athletes can keep injuries to a minimum.

Prevention of accidents, however, is everyone's responsibility. It is the duty of the instructor, the coach, the administrator, the fencer, medical and maintenance personnel, and everyone connected in one way or another with fencing to be constantly safety-conscious.

Before injuries occur, it is the responsibility of the concerned administrators of the institution to see that the instructor or coach, the athletic trainers, and the institutional medical personnel are trained to provide timely care and service to injured athletes. Every supervisor in the fencing program should be prepared to summon trained medical help from the most appropriate source: the school health service, the team or school physician or trainer, or the local emergency operations center or ambulance service. At least one member of the coaching or teaching staff should be qualified to provide initial care while waiting for trained medical help to arrive, and, specifically, to be currently certified in first aid by a recognized agency such as the American Red Cross.

Providing adequate safety measures is a major task for institutions involved in varsity sports and athletic programs. Today every coach and sports instructor must function as a "reasonable and prudent professional" in accordance with the legal interpretation established in lawsuits involving sports participants who suffered injuries. Care must be taken by the fencing instructor/coach to avoid any hint of negligence.

PREVENTING MISHAPS

Very few events labeled accidents are really accidents in the sense of being purely chance events. For example, in one collegiate meet a regulation strip (mat) was used.

Before the competition began, the mat had not been properly cleaned and the surface was therefore unsafe for bouting. As a result, one fencer tore a hamstring muscle when he lunged. The cause was identifiable; the event was foreseeable and preventable.

Such unfortunate things happen because people often lack foresight and make mistakes. Consequently, when an "accident" is attributable to "human error," coaches or instructors may find themselves being charged with negligence.

If the cause of an incident was known to exist, that incident is not an accident. We should not cultivate a philosophy of carelessness and irresponsibility by labeling all unpleasant surprises as "accidents." We must remember that administrators, instructors, coaches, officials, and/or participating fencers all share in the responsibility for the mishaps that occur.

AREAS OF CONCERN IN PREVENTING FENCING INJURIES

Fencing Surfaces

The portion of the field of play used for fencing is called the strip, the mat, or the piste. The strip may be of rubber, wood, linoleum, cork, plastic, metal, metal mesh, asphalt, or concrete.

USFA rules require that a host institution must inform visiting teams of the type of surface to be used. The athletes then select the most appropriate and safest footwear.

If the strip is placed on a platform, regulation prohibits it from being more than 0.5 meters high. The strip should be extended at each end by 1.5 to 2.0 meters, to allow the fencer crossing the rear limit to retreat over an even and unbroken surface.

All strips should be secured to prevent the mat from shifting, wrinkling, and/or buckling. This may be accomplished by taping the mat to the floor using tape 3 or 4 inches wide (preferably duct tape).

Proper Layout of Fencing Strips in the Gymnasium

Fencing requires ample space for mobility and for freedom from obstacles. In order to eliminate interference from other participants, the lines of activity should be parallel. (See the recommended layouts.) In tournaments, the strip should be arranged so that fencers and officials have easy access.

For each strip, the minimum floor area (excluding passageways or spectator seats) should be 56 feet (about 17 meters) long and 18 feet (about 5.5 meters) wide, or approximately 1,008 square feet (about 93.5 square meters) per strip.

The floors and strips should be thoroughly cleaned and dry-mopped as often as necessary.

All fencing areas should be free from obstructions likely to cause injury.

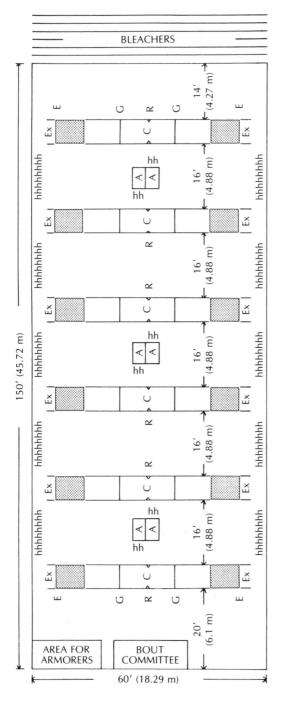

Legend: Shaded area = Warning area

A = Table for scoring machine
C = Center of strip
G = On-guard lines
Ex = Strip extension for safety
R = Referee
E = End limit, all weapons
hhh = Chairs for fencers and/or scorekeepers and timekeepers

A Recommended Strip Layout for a Tournament in a Rectangular Floor Area

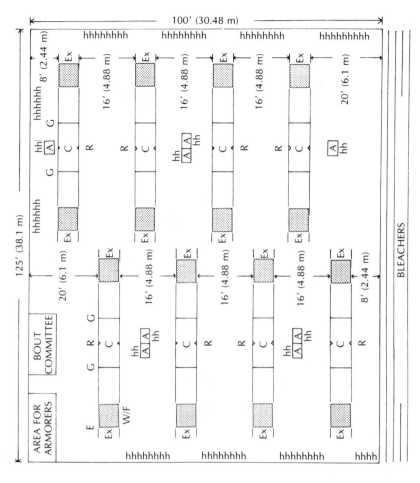

Legend:

Shaded area = Warning area

A = Table for scoring machine
C = Center of strip
G = On-guard lines
Ex = Strip extension for safety
R = Referee
E = End limit, all weapons
hhh = Chairs for fencers and/or scorekeepers and timekeepers

A Recommended Strip Layout for a Tournament in a Square Floor Area

Space

Insufficient space between the sidelines of the play area and the walls or the bleachers is a common hazard. When such distances cannot be widened, steps should be taken to pad the walls or otherwise eliminate the hazard.

Wherever possible, all fencing strips should be roped off to prevent interference from spectators.

Environmental Factors

The fencing area should be well ventilated and well lighted. Changes in air flow, temperature, or humidity call for adjustments in the body to maintain a body temperature of 98.6°F (36.6°C). The two prime temperature-regulating mechanisms in the body are the sweat glands and the blood vessels. As the environmental temperature nears 80.6°F (27°C), the blood vessels contract and expand, the primary means of controlling body-heat loss through the skin. The unfortunate aspect of having the blood vessels fully dilated is that nearly half the blood is diverted from the deep body tissue and mental processes to the skin areas and then returns to the heart. Consequently, heat stress is a great strain on the heart, and mental functions tend to deteriorate in high temperatures.*

Owing to the physiological effects of temperature changes on the human body, neither comfort nor maximum efficiency is achieved with excessively high room-air temperatures. For an optimum environment with maximum learning efficiency in a practice area, it is recommended that an air temperature of 65° to 68°F (18.3° to 20°C) be maintained.

Factors that could adversely affect visual accuracy should be corrected. Glare control, uniformity of light intensity, and adequate illumination can affect both performance and safety. Prevention of glare is accomplished by use of shields and louvers on light sources and by avoiding high-gloss surface finishes. (Uniformity of light intensity refers to the even distribution of lumens across the fencing area to enhance visibility.) Thirty to 80 foot-candles of illumination are recommended.** The instrument used to measure the candle power of any light source is called a photometer.

Fencing Equipment

Proper equipment and supplies are necessary for safe performance by the competitors. Equipment and supplies are usually divided into permanent and expendable categories.

*Per-Olof Astrand, M.D., and Kaare Rodahl, M.D., *Textbook of Work Physiology* (New York: McGraw-Hill Book Company, 1970), pp. 491–536.

**Kenneth A Penman, *Planning Physical Education and Athletic Facilities in Schools* (New York: John Wiley and Sons, 1977), pp. 183–84. One foot-candle is equal to one lumen per square foot.

Permanent equipment usually does not need replacement until after several years of use: fencing strips (mats), bleachers, tools, public address system, scoreboard, and the like.

Expendable equipment is that which must be replaced regularly due to wear. This category includes fencing masks, uniforms and shoes, weapons and blades, and electronic recording apparatus and reels.

The importance of good-quality equipment cannot be overemphasized. The very nature of fencing suggests the element of danger, so there is a great need for sturdy, safe, and durable equipment. Regular and careful maintenance is extremely important too.

Catalogs and price lists from equipment manufacturers and dealers are helpful in comparing quality, prices, and equipment specifications. Addresses for these manufacturers can be obtained from the USFA and the USFCA.

PHYSICAL PREPAREDNESS AND CONDITIONING

The instructor or coach has final responsibility for the physical preparedness of the fencers. This responsibility is shared with the administration of the institution and the assigned medical personnel.

Medical Clearance

All fencers should have an annual medical checkup and clearance before participating in practice and contests. The medical examination should be performed by a licensed physician.

Medical Information

Medical records must be maintained for all participants and should include the date and place of physical examination, the name of the examining physician, the kind of examination performed, and a listing of medical information in case of emergency. This information should be kept on file and readily available to the instructor or coach (see suggested medical information form).

Athletes who have remediable defects and therefore do not pass the medical examination should receive the therapy necessary to restore them to good condition. It is the athlete's responsibility to follow through with the prescribed remedial program.

Distinctive physical characteristics and/or medical problems should be discussed with athletes (or parents/guardians of minors). The instructor should review the medical report with each fencer (and/or a parent/guardian) to ensure that everyone will fully understand the element of risk from physical and psychological factors.

If eyeglasses are required, a mask should be fitted so that glasses can be worn comfortably and vision will not be hindered. Safety lenses and frames or contact lenses may be recommended. Allergies, chronic ailments, excessive fatigue or weakness, and abnormal body weight are among other factors to consider. Specialists should be consulted about corrective measures, including improved diet. An instructor or coach should not assume the responsibilities of a physician, trainer, or nutritionist.

Consent, Waiver, and Release Forms

Require consent, waiver, and release forms, and keep them on file.

> A consent form should be on file for every participant, signed by a parent or legal guardian if the participant is a minor, or by the participant. The form should contain a waiver of claims against the sponsor and staff of the program for any aggravation of a pre-existing condition, or for any injury resulting from that condition. The form should also release the program sponsor and staff from responsibility for any injury occurring during the program. Consent, waiver, and release forms are frequently prescribed by education institutions and athletic associations or clubs. It should be recognized that . . . the participant consents only to the normal risks of the sport, and that in signing a form [the participant] does not waive the right to sue for negligence. The supervising instructor/coach should consult a lawyer in case of doubt about the forms.*

A Testing and Evaluation Program

The measure of a fencer's physical preparedness is determined by the ability to perform basic skills with good balance, form, rhythm, technique, and endurance. Fundamental skills include: stance (on-guard); grasp (grip) of the weapon; hand positions with the weapon; mobility exercises with or without the weapon in hand—advance, retreat, lunge, balestra, redoublement, recovery from the lunge, the flèche, and combinations of these movements; fencing distance; parries; attacks; and counterattacks.

Mastering these skills prepares a student for the next level: novice competition. A fencer may then progress to higher competitive levels. Progress can be measured by comparative evaluations with other fencers and by performance in competitions.

Warm-up

Athletes should participate in appropriate conditioning (warm-up) exercises before every skill session. All athletes should be thoroughly warmed up before performing strenuously or competing. The warm-up process is different for each individual and is not the same in all weather conditions. A carefully developed warm-up program should be designed to fit each fencer's individual needs.

*Eugene Wettstone, ed., Gymnastics Safety Manual, 2nd ed. (University Park: The Pennsylvania State University Press, 1979), pp. 41–42.

Participant _____   _____ _____
                           (name)   (age)   (sex)

Physical Handicaps   Psychological Handicaps
(Specify missing or injured body   (Specify problem areas such as anxieties,
parts, weaknesses, etc.)   fears, hyperactivity, hypersensitivity.)

bones and joints _____   _____

muscles _____   _____

organs _____   _____

weight problem _____   _____

Chronic Ailments   Allergies
asthma, or other respiratory problems   insect bites _____

_____   tetanus shots _____

circulatory or heart problems   other, if significant _____

_____   _____

diabetes or hypoglycemia _____   Blood type _____

epilepsy _____   Current Medication (if any)

hemophilia, or other bleeding problems   _____

_____

Physician Who Conducted Examination

_____ _____   _____
        (name)   (phone no.)   (date of latest examination)

Preferred Personal or Family Physician(s)   Health Insurance (if any)

_____ _____   _____
        (name)   (phone no.)   (name of insuror)

_____ _____   _____
        (name)   (phone no.)   (policy no.)

Parent(s), Guardian(s), or Other Relatives Employer (if any)

_____ _____   _____
        (name)   (phone no.)   (name)

_____ _____   _____
        (name)   (phone no.)   (phone no.)

_____ _____
        (name)   (phone no.)

A Form for Medical Information

All athletes should systematically warm up each major body area before starting skill-training sessions:

For head and arms: rubber-ball squeeze, push-ups, pull-ups (chins), dips on parallel bars, flexion and extension of arms with adjustable weights.

For neck and shoulders: neck rotations, arm-swinging, arm-crossing, arm-and-shoulder rotations.

For feet: ankle rotations, ankle (Achilles tendon) stretching.

For legs: stretching thigh and calf muscles using hurdler's position, leg-swinging, leg rotations, knee lifting, squatting, walking on tiptoe, walking in a crouch, hopping on both feet forward and backward (to the left and to the right), straddle-hopping, stride-hopping, rope-skipping, jogging, sprinting.

For rib cage: trunk-twisting, trunk-bending, trunk-leaning.

For back: trunk lifts from prone position, leg lifts from prone position, trunk and leg lifts from prone position.

For abdomen: trunk-bending backward, trunk-twisting, leg and knee lifts, bicycle exercise from back lying position, sit-ups with knees flexed.

For lungs: breathing exercises.

PROGRESSION FOR TEACHING FENCING SKILLS

The activities and teaching procedures should be organized to help the student pass through a progression of skills, as outlined in this book. Particular care should be given to skill areas with the greatest incidence of injuries, such as lunging (muscle pulls and/or strains), balestra, sprinting, and running (shin splints, heel bruises, tendonitis).

Just as the success of a team or individual depends upon the acquisition of skills, so does the safety of individuals depend to a great extent upon mastery of good safety practices. Coaches and instructors should therefore be thorough and meticulous in the instruction of fundamental skills in both fencing and safety.

ADEQUATE STAFF SUPERVISION

All activities, including free or open fencing periods, should be supervised by the teaching and/or coaching staff at all times. Liability appears to hinge greatly upon the question of supervision—the degree and character of such supervision, as well as the competence of the supervising personnel. Courts have increasingly held that athletic supervisors are responsible for inspecting the environment and equipment as well as the activity. Supervisory personnel must therefore carefully inspect the area of play to see that hazardous obstacles are removed and that protective equipment and gear are safe. They should also be aware of physiological and psychological stresses that might lead to undue fatigue.

Many variables make it difficult to specify an exact numerical ratio of fencers to instructors/coaches: the ages of the fencers, the teaching methods, the amount of teaching experience, the skill levels of the fencers, the equipment being used, and the physical characteristics of the instructional facility. However, the personal experiences of the authors have led them to develop the following guide as a recommendation for the ratio of fencers to instructors/coaches/supervisors in group instruction:

Age of Students	Number of Students per Instructor/Coach/Supervisor
12 & under	5–10
13–17	10–15
18 +	8–12 (in PE class, up to 24)

SAFETY AWARENESS

The development of safety awareness is fundamental to all areas of responsibility. This includes the establishment of good safety attitudes, a thorough knowledge of the factors involved in safety, and the development of the necessary skills for safe participation in the sport.

Attitudes

A safety-conscious attitude in sports is essential if the frequency and severity of injuries in fencing are to be reduced. Everyone who is directly or indirectly involved with the sport of fencing—competitors, coaches, instructors, officials, administrators, equipment manufacturers, maintenance personnel, physicians, athletic trainers, and parents—should become safety-conscious. To inculcate a favorable attitude permitting fencers to enjoy participation in a safe and healthful manner, everyone must have an understanding of (1) the factors and conditions that can lead to accidents, (2) the principles and practices of accident prevention, and (3) the responsibilities of all individuals participating in fencing.

It is essential that the fencer develop the ability to make sound judgments and rational choices with respect to the manner of participation and performance.

Awareness

Accident prevention in fencing demands a constant awareness of contributing factors—mechanical, physiological, environmental, and psychological.

Physiological factors include such items as physical condition, fatigue, lack of concentration, and the effects of alcohol or drugs on the athlete.

Environmental factors include temperature, humidity, lighting, noise, and physical and architectural barriers.

Psychological factors to consider include emotional reactions to fencing tactics, the attitude and temperament of coaches/instructors and competitors, and the atmosphere created by officials conducting the bout or tournament. The development of courtesy and good sportsmanship is as important as success in competition.

Sound attitudes must be supplemented by knowledge and techniques to counteract hazards, whether physiological, environmental, or psychological. To achieve a significant degree of safety, fencers should be able to recognize, control, and remove hazards, and avoid creating additional hazards.

Emphasizing Safety with the Basic Skills

Since we tend to enjoy most that which we do well, it is essential that the student receive proper instruction in the basic skills with an emphasis on safety. Developing the basic skills allows for participation in fencing with a high degree of competence, success, and pleasure. Toward this end the instructor/coach should:

Insist on adequate warm-up and conditioning exercises before bouting.

Help students develop an awareness of correct general position of the arms and legs in relation to the body when on-guard, in the lunge, in the flèche, or in any of the other fencing positions, to prevent bad habits leading to injuries.

Concentrate on having students assume the proper posture for all fencing positions.

Teach proper landing of the lead foot when lunging, thereby avoiding heel bruises.

Teach the correct action of the rear leg when recovering from a lunge.

Practice proper footwork (advance, retreat, balestra, lunge, flèche, and their variations), emphasizing balance, rhythm, and sense of distance to avoid hazardous situations leading to injuries.

Establish a sound teaching progression of the fencing skills.

Further the development of the student's tactile, auditory, and visual reactions through simulated competitive drills.

Emphasize the correct response to equipment failure—for example, learn to flex the elbow of the weapon arm immediately upon completion of an attack, especially if the blade breaks.

The Safety Awareness Checklist printed here is intended only as a guide and does not pretend to be complete. Readers are encouraged to make any appropriate additions.

SAFETY AWARENESS CHECKLIST

Environmental:
1. Is the strip (mat) secure, clean, and safe for instruction and performance?
2. Is the fencing area free of obstruction?
3. Is the protective equipment (masks, fencing jackets, gloves, underarm protectors) in good condition?

4. Are the weapons safe for use?
5. Is there adequate lighting?
6. Is the room temperature set at a comfortable and safe level for the participants?

Individual:
1. Is the fencer in good health?
2. Is the fencer prepared physically and mentally for instruction in a new skill? Balance? Flexibility? Endurance? Coordination? Warm-up? Strength? Motivation?
3. Has the fencer any fear or anxiety that may interfere with the safe performance of the skill?
4. Has the fencer attained sufficient mastery of the required preliminary skills?

Instructor:
1. Is the instructor competently prepared and does he or she have sufficient knowledge of the mechanics of the skill to be taught?
2. Is the instructor aware of the individual differences of each fencer and of the learning sequence to meet each fencer's needs?
3. Is the instructor able to make adjustments in teaching strategy to accommodate each fencer's individual level of achievement?
4. Is the instructor capable of analyzing the errors in a fencer's performance and making the necessary adjustments or corrections?

The major responsibility is that of properly preparing an athlete in a safe environment, disciplining the individual to perform skills safely, developing sound, wholesome, and acceptable attitudes, and understanding factors that cause accidents or injuries.

To achieve a significant degree of safety, the fencers, teachers, and coaches should be able to recognize, control, and avoid creating hazards.

FENCING SAFETY RULES

Fencing safety is everyone's responsibility.

1. Do not fence without the required protective equipment.
2. Use proper conditioning and warm-up exercises before beginning a vigorous workout or competition.
3. Check the strip, the electrical equipment, and the area for hazardous or unsafe conditions.
4. Practice and compete only under qualified supervision; check with the instructor/coach.
5. Adhere to established rules and regulations of the Fédération Internationale d'Escrime.
6. Refrain from and prohibit theatricals or horseplay in practice or competitive areas.

Enforcement of Safety Measures

The Fédération Internationale d'Escrime (FIE) has developed rules for fencing that also provide safety procedures. These are set forth in *Fencing Rules—Authorized English Translation of the International (FIE) Rules.** It is mandatory that everyone concerned with fencing (coaches, instructors, officials, manufacturers, and fencers) be thoroughly familiar with these rules. Individual fencers should be particularly concerned with the rules pertaining to personal equipment and clothing.

It is the responsibility of the instructor/coach and the individual fencer to adhere to the rules designed for the performer's safety, and it is the responsibility of the officials to check each fencer and to enforce these safety standards before any bout begins.

TRAINING OF QUALIFIED EXPERTS

A major function of the United States Fencing Coaches Association (USFCA) has been to upgrade the competency of the fencing teacher through a process of testing, certifying, and accrediting fencing instructors, prevosts, and masters. The Accreditation and Certification Board of the U.S. Fencing Coaches Association is the examining body for coaches and instructors who want to be rated as Fencing Instructor (in one weapon), Prevost (in all three weapons), or Fencing Master (in all three weapons). The examinations for each diploma include:

For Instructor: Taking and giving lessons; conducting a group lesson; directing; fencing. Written examination.

For Prevost and Master: Written, oral, and practical examinations. Those interested in applying for accreditation can do so by writing to the United States Academy of Arms, Accreditation/Certification Board, in care of the U.S. Fencing Coaches Association.

CERTIFYING OFFICIALS

Certification of officials is an ongoing program sponsored by the USFA. The Fencing Officials Commission appointed by the USFA is the official body designated to develop trained referees (formerly directors or presidents). This program is accomplished by means of clinics, seminars, demonstrations, and other similar means. The Fencing Officials Commission (FOC) also establishes the standards and criteria for certifying such officials.

Candidates who want to become referees must pass both written and practical examinations. The practical examination takes into account five criteria: mechanics, decisiveness, poise, analysis of fencing actions, and the ability to apply appropriate rules. Anyone wishing to apply for an official's rating can do so by writing or calling the Fencing Officials Commission (FOC), appointed by the USFA.

*Translated by Joseph A. Byrnes.

ORGANIZATION AND POLICY

Among everyone concerned with fencing, there is a significant trend toward emphasizing accident-prevention. This is evident in the growing attention to:

Safety education.
Licensing, certification, and registration programs for fencing masters and officials.
Enforcement of fencing rules and regulations.
Thorough conditioning programs.
Proper environment and equipment.
The importance of "progression" in skill development.

Those who administer sports programs should regard safety as a major responsibility in their cooperative relationship with all personnel.

A Policy Committee

Establishing a policy committee concerned with safety is an effective way to educate
and motivate personnel. It is a fine method for developing cooperation, exchanging
ideas, and developing good safety attitudes, practices, and knowledge. There are
various ways to organize such a committee. Here is a typical structure:

```
┌───── ADMINISTRATOR (CHAIRPERSON) ─────┐
```

MEMBERSHIP	AGENDA
Business manager	Accident report, with charts
Equipment supervisor	Safety standing, with charts
Grounds maintenance supervisor	Lost time from classes, practices, and
Head coaches	competitions due to accidents or in-
Head trainer	juries report, with charts
Team physician	Establishment of safety practices and
Safety policy committee	policies
	New assignments
	Membership and agenda

Safety Policy Committee—Membership and Agenda

SAFETY INDOCTRINATION

It is essential that a safety indoctrination program be held for all beginning fencers.
The program should stress the importance of avoiding self-caused injuries due to
unsafe protective equipment or the lack of proper conditioning. It should also stress

prevention of possible injury to opponents due to unsportsmanlike or illegal fencing tactics and unskilled practices.

Failure to take proper precautions might be cause for a legal claim. Quite apart from the legal liability involved, it is morally disagreeable to realize your opponent has sustained a serious injury due to your negligence.

LEARNING EXPERIENCE

1. Attend a fencing tournament. Carefully note the safety precautions taken or disregarded by the referees on each strip.
2. List the safety measures you take in training and in competition.
3. Indicate the safety procedures you would follow if a serious accident were to occur where you practice.

HIGHLIGHTS

1. Define the term "accident."
2. List the individuals who are responsible for seeing that mishaps do not occur.
3. Design the layout of your gymnasium for a tournament of thirty-six fencers.
4. Check the equipment in your program to ensure that safety standards are met.
5. Find out from your trainer and/or physician how many and what type of fencing injuries they treat.

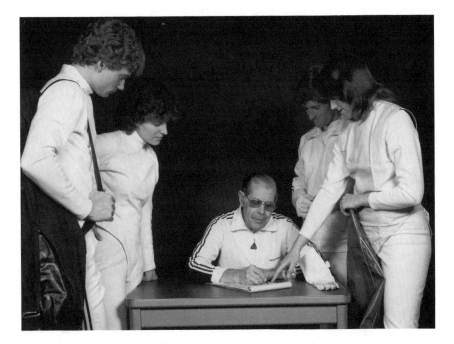

12

Liability and Negligence
By Steve Sobel, President and Former Counsel of the United States Fencing Association

Avoid injuries, avoid lawsuits. The practical approach to legal responsibility is to stay out of court. To do this requires careful planning, the exercise of reasonable care, a knowledge of the law, and an understanding of the risks involved.

Anyone can sue anybody for anything, so there is no way to completely eliminate the possibility of a lawsuit. And once you are sued, you are a loser. Even if you win the case and are not liable to pay damages to the plaintiff, the victory will be pyrrhic, earned after years of litigation, hours of preparation, adverse publicity, and thousands of dollars in legal fees and disbursements.

It is costly both to sue and to be sued, but there is one major difference. Defense attorneys earn their fees whether they win or lose. The plaintiff's attorney is usually retained for a contingent fee. He earns only a percentage of the money collected, and nothing if he loses. This distinction creates peculiar economic conclusions apart from the merits of any case.

There will not usually be a lawsuit unless there is a good chance to win and collect a large award. Once the suit is initiated, everyone remotely involved will be sued, because the cost to join additional defendants is relatively insignificant and bringing them in substantially increases the probability of success. One major injury in sports can therefore result in a million-dollar lawsuit against the opponent, coach, official, owner of the gymnasium or athletic facility, sponsor of the tournament, equipment manufacturers, physicians, and trainers who render aid at the scene. As a potential defendant, your chance of being sued decreases if the injuries suffered are minor or if the liability is questionable.

Every case has a nuisance value for purposes of settlement. It is cheaper for a defendant not to contest a claim if he can pay the plaintiff anything less than the cost of defending the lawsuit, since this cost has to be paid anyway and payment avoids the risk of losing the case. The plaintiff is encouraged to settle because there is always the possibility of losing everything, and even if the plaintiff wins he can face years of paying out money he doesn't have for the legal costs of the trial and appeal and for the medical costs of treatment. Pretrial tactics often involve increasing the cost and inconvenience to the adversary by court motions, depositions, and expensive discovery procedures, in the hope of achieving an economic surrender of the party least able to afford the costs.

Avoiding litigation therefore involves two basic concepts: minimizing the risk and expense of being sued, and exercising the standard of care necessary to avoid liability.

MINIMIZING THE RISK AND EXPENSE OF BEING SUED

Liability Insurance

The most effective method for avoiding litigation expense is to carry liability insurance, since it pays the expense of the litigation as well as any damages awarded. Ironically, however, it may increase the risk of being sued because it guarantees that money will be available to pay any judgment award. Nevertheless, if this coverage is available at a reasonable cost, be sure to have it.

If you don't have specific liability insurance, inquire about being covered. Sometimes coverage is possible by paying a small additional premium on an existing multiperil or umbrella policy. Sometimes organizations offer coverage to members that can be obtained for a very low premium. Many physical education instructors may be eligible for coverage with the American Alliance for Health, Physical Education and Recreation, and Dance (AAHPER-D) or with the National Recreation and

Park Association (NRPA). Often an employer, university, or sponsor of a particular program may have a policy that will cover the risk. Look into all possibilities and coverage available at the most reasonable price.

The Waiver of Liability

Parents and institutions involved in the sponsoring and operating fencing programs will be wise to require participants, and their parents/guardians if they are minors, to sign a waiver of liability form, which should include risks connected with team travel and emergency medical care as well as injuries incurred during participation. These waivers are not absolute defenses because many courts hold them unenforceable for a variety of legal reasons, but there is nothing to lose by obtaining them. It can do no harm, and it often discourages people from bringing lawsuits.

Public Relations

Do not underestimate the value of good public relations as an effective precaution against lawsuits. Demonstrate legitimate concern for the athletes, and provide prompt attention when an injury occurs. This practice might prevent lawsuits that are started by angry litigants, not for the purpose of obtaining reimbursement damages but to avenge a presumed injustice or insult.

AVOIDING LIABILITY BY EXERCISING REASONABLE CARE

Liability is based on negligence, which is the failure to exercise reasonable and prudent care. It must be noted that the fencing instructor/coach must act as a reasonable and prudent professional.

Whether this obligation was fulfilled is usually a question the jury must make based on the facts of each case. Because two different juries can reach opposite decisions on the same facts, there is always uncertainty. Nevertheless, previous cases have provided general guidelines that are worth careful consideration. Chapter 11 of this book, "Safety," tells what constitutes safety in fencing—appropriate fencing surfaces, proper layout of strips in the gymnasium, equipment that complies with FIE safety rules, competent supervision, and adequate emergency care. This chapter emphasizes the legal aspect of the qualification "reasonable" as it pertains to these facts.

Competent Supervision

The personnel in charge must be competent and must exercise the control and supervision required. The more inexperienced the student, the greater the required supervision. An official at a tournament may be negligent in permitting fencing in his or her presence without the use of safety equipment required by the rules. A coach or instructor has a greater responsibility—to instruct and inform the students and to require that immature or inexperienced pupils fence only when they can be observed and supervised by trained instructors. Let's look at a few specific examples:

Is it necessary to supervise students while they are warming up?

At intercollegiate matches, the coach usually observes the bouts in progress while the on-deck fencers often warm up without supervision, sometimes in another room. Because college varsity fencers are mature individuals who have received instructions on the proper safety practices and acceptable warm-up methods, and because this described practice happens to be common, a coach who permits it is probably exercising reasonable care under the circumstances.

At the high school level and among inexperienced or immature fencers, a trained supervisor should be in attendance during warm-up sessions. This does not mean that all high school varsity fencers are immature or inexperienced. Many high school students are mature individuals and are world-class fencers who have won national championships and compete on international teams. However, because local boards of education usually require supervision, failure to supervise creates an issue that can support a jury's finding of negligence. It is therefore wiser to follow the established standard instead of creating your own.

Should coaches give lessons to students not wearing masks and jackets?

I have insulted the pride of some coaches by absolutely prohibiting all warm-up lessons at USFA competitions unless both the coach and the student wear a mask and jacket. It is my opinion that lessons without proper equipment are unnecessary, unwise, and unsafe at all times. The USFA cannot enforce proper safety procedures at private clubs. At USFA competitions, no fencing or lessons are permitted unless proper equipment is worn, and I strongly recommend this standard wherever fencing takes place.

Should a fencer compete after an injury?

Who is responsible for making this decision? The supervisor must always exercise reasonable care and is therefore responsible for the decision. However, decisions requiring expertise that supervisors do not have should be based on the opinions of experts.

Fencers should be required to get competent medical advice and submit a written report from their physicians concerning their complete recovery from any previous serious injury or illness. At a competition or practice, someone with adequate emergency and first-aid training and planned emergency access to medical assistance should be available. The supervisor must determine whether a trainer is adequate or a physician is required, which will depend on the nature of the accident and the facts of the particular case.

The important lesson to be learned from the above illustrations is that you must make safety decisions regularly. What constitutes reasonable and prudent professional care is not always clear, and if an injury results there will be many Monday morning critics reviewing your decision. If in doubt, it is better to be cautious than sorry. Your primary purpose is to avoid injuries and lawsuits, not to exercise merely the minimum care necessary to win a case.

Put safety instructions in writing. All safety instructions should be in writing and distributed to the fencers for two reasons. First, in the event someone did not hear or understand the instructions, the written material serves as repetition or clarification. Second, the written document is evidence that safety instructions were provided to the participants in the program. If written safety instructions are violated, the individual is then at fault for failure to follow them, but without the written document the violation is difficult to prove.

Safe Equipment

Reasonable care requires the use of equipment that complies with the rules. Underarm protectors, masks, and jackets must be in good condition. Throw out old and frayed masks and jackets. The cost of one lawsuit could pay for all the replacement equipment you would ever plan to buy.

Safe Facilities

Reasonable care requires adequate space, lighting, and security. Fencing strips should be of satisfactory material, not too close to each other, and not too close to dangerous obstructions, such as pillars, doorways, or windows.

Student Athlete Responsibility

Student athletes should be constantly reminded of the relationship between fencing procedures and safety rules, and likewise of their shared responsibility in protecting themselves, their teammates, and their opponents.

ACCESS TO EMERGENCY CARE

Whether an injury is minor or major often depends on the emergency care rendered at the scene. Advance planning must include knowledge of appropriate emergency procedures, the availability of trained personnel, and immediate access to essential first-aid equipment. Emergency procedures should be routinely practiced, like fire drills.

CONCLUSIONS

The primary purpose of this chapter is to present general advice in the legal aspects of planning a fencing program. Therefore, specific legal theories available as defenses to lawsuits but not pertinent to the planning of a program—such as statutes of limitation, assumption of the risk, proximate cause, and contributory negligence—are beyond the scope of the chapter and have not been discussed.

A general discussion of this type is not a substitute for specific advice. You should consult attorneys, physicians, and insurance agents, as well as experienced fencers and coaches. If you need technical advice on fencing, or the recommendation of competent personnel, this information is available at no charge from the USFA or the USFCA. Advice is available for the asking. Do not neglect to ask.

The proliferation of consumer litigation against professionals for malpractice, against manufacturers for product liability, and against anyone for negligence places everyone in a very precarious position. Although you have no obligation to volunteer, you must exercise reasonable care once you do so. This means you must plan ahead, act carefully, and seek advice in order to make correct and reasonable decisions according to the facts of each case. Your emphasis should be to plan a safe fencing program for everyone to enjoy. By achieving this, you will also avoid injuries and lawsuits, at the same time.

LEARNING EXPERIENCE

1. Are you personally covered by health and accident insurance? What is the extent of your insurance coverage? Are others covered by your policy?
2. Does your institution provide for liability, health, and/or accident insurance? What is the extent of this coverage?
3. What safety procedures do you follow when taking a lesson?
4. Study the waiver-of-liability form used at your institution. Do you believe it is comprehensive and informative?

HIGHLIGHTS

1. List the two basic concepts for avoiding litigation.
2. Define negligence.
3. Prepare a poster listing safety rules and regulations to be observed in your practice and competition areas.

Glossary and Index

Absence of Blades.   The situation in which the opponents' blades are not in contact. 43, 136

Accelerometer.   *See* Sensor.

Advance.   A forward movement of the body executed by moving the leading foot first and following with the rear foot (without crossing the feet). The opposite of retreat. 30, 31, 89, 124

Aids (fingers).   The last three fingers (middle, ring, small) of the weapon hand. *Compare* Manipulators. 15, 25

Archer Tandy.   *See* Socket.

Attack.   A simple or compound aggressive action. 41, 48, 57, 58, 60, 87, 89, 90, 99, 128

Attack in Time.   *See* Stop Hit.

Attention Position.   The fencer stands erect with feet at right angles, as in the diagram on page 26. The weapon arm is extended with the weapon pointed diagonally downward and forward and with the point just slightly off the floor. The mask is cradled by the rear arm with the meshwork facing forward. 26

Balestra.   A method of attack that employs a jump forward with the lunge. 55, 71, 89, 124, 125

Barrage.   A fence-off due to a tie. 159

Beat.   A sharp, controlled blow against the middle or weak part of the opponent's blade. 45, 46, 94, 95

Beat Attack.   An attack in which the fencer's weapon strikes the opponent's blade to deflect it before launching the final offensive movement. 49, 93, 94, 95

Bell Guard.   The metallic part of the weapon—circular and convex in foil and épée, and elliptical and convex as in saber—that protects the hand. Also known as the *coquille*. 10, 12, 15, 16, 69, 113, 114, 177

Bind.   Taking of the blade from high line to low line or vice versa. Compare *Croisé*. 50, 129

Blade.   All blades are made of flexible steel. The cross section of the foil blade is quadrangular; the épée blade is triangular in section without cutting edges; the saber blade is approximately rectangular in section. The maximum length of the foil and épée blades forward of the bell guard is 90 cm; for saber it is 88 cm. 10, 12, 14, 68, 113, 114, 176

Body Cord.   The electrical wiring cord worn by the fencer, which connects the weapon to the electrical apparatus. 16, 69, 71, 115, 172, 177, 178

Bout.   The formal personal combat between two fencers. See Fencing Bout. To engage in a bout. 12, 116, 149, 150, 151

Bout Line   An imaginary straight line that would pass from the rear heel through the front foot of one fencer, continuing through the front foot to the rear heel of the opponent as they face each other in the fencing position. 29, 37, 77, 119

Bout Plane.   An imaginary two-dimensional plane that arises from the bout line perpendicular to the fencing strip. 29, 75, 76, 83

Button.   The extremity of the blade, flat at the tip of the foil and the épée. In the electric foil and épée, the button (tip) is called the *point*. In saber, the end of the blade must be folded over onto itself or be fashioned in one piece to form a button, which—viewed end on—must have a square or rectangular cross section of 4 mm minimum and 6 mm maximum. The maximum dimension must be not more than 3 mm from the end of the blade. 12, 14, 68, 113, 114

Cadence.   A fencing rhythm. 30, 31, 144

Change Beat.   A beat executed by a change of engagement. 50

Change of Engagement.   The act of engaging in a new line. 43, 44, 45

Close.   To defend a line of engagement against a straight thrust. 37, 38

Closed Line.   A line of engagement when the defender's weapon has covered or closed the line to a straight thrust. 37, 38

Corps-à-Corps.   Said to exist when two competitors are in contact, at which point the referee must stop the bout. 127, 152

Coulé.   The French term for a *glide*, which is a thrust in the line of engagement while keeping contact with the opponent's blade. 50, 129

Counter-time Actions.   Movements of second intention. 64, 65, 109, 110

Coupé Attack.   The French term for cutover. 43, 128, 134, 135

Croisé.   A blade-taking action that carries the opposing weapon from a high line to a low line, on the same side as the engagement. 50, 51, 129

Cross-Advance.   The crossing of the rear foot ahead of the front foot as the body weight shifts forward. 56, 71, 72, 92

Cross-Retreat.   The crossing of the front foot behind the rear foot as the body weight shifts backward. 71, 72

Cuissard.   The portion of a fencing jacket that protects the groin area. 17

Cut.   A movement utilizing the "cutting edge" of the saber blade with which to score a hit. The cut may be directed to the arm, head, flank, chest, or belly— all valid target areas in saber. 80, 81, 82, 83, 84, 85

Cutover.   A form of disengage that passes over the point of the opposing blade. 43, 61, 128, 134, 135

Deceiving the Blade.   An action that consists of removing one's blade from an opponent's attempt to make contact with it. 48, 52, 101, 103, 104, 105

Deceiving the Parry.   An offensive action consisting of avoiding the opponent's attempt to block the attacking blade. 48, 101, 103, 104, 105

Direct Attack (Simple).   A single-blade action into the line of engagement. 41, 42, 128

Octave (8th).   The position that covers (protects) the low outside line. The hand is supinated, with the point lower than the hand. 38, 58, 59, 120

On Deck.   The next pair of scheduled adversaries ready to compete when the bout in progress is completed. 161

One-Two Attack.   This attack involves two disengages. The first disengage is a feint designed to draw a direct (lateral) parry, the second disengage is to deceive the intended parry. 60, 128

On-Guard.   The fundamental position of the fencer preparing to bout. 27, 28, 29, 71, 75, 118

Open Line(s).   Unprotected area(s) or position(s). 37, 38, 44

Open Target.   An unprotected target area. 93, 98, 99

Opposition.   A movement of taking and retaining the opponent's blade. 129, 133, 134

Orthopedic Handle.   The term applied to molded handles. 15, 16, 23, 114

Overload Principle.   A gradual progressive increase in resistance that will tend to strengthen muscles, enabling them to react with greater force. 165

Pad.   A cushion or padding located inside the bell guard. 12, 15, 70

Parry.   A defensive action made with the weapon to deflect the attacker's blade. To take such action. 38, 45, 46, 47, 58, 59, 95–99, 104

Phrase.   An uninterrupted exchange of blade actions, ending either with a touch or with the fencers breaking off the action. Also known as *phrase d'armes*. 156, 157

Piste.   The strip or mat. 12, 149, 175, 178, 182, 183, 187

Pistol Handle.   *See* Orthopedic Handle.

Plastron.   An undergarment worn to protect the armpit and side. 12, 17, 172

Point Control.   The correct execution of blade movements, keeping the point in line while threatening the opponent's target. 132, 133

Point-in-Line.   Refers to weapon arm being extended with point toward opponent's target. 105, 108

Pommel.   A metal piece at the rear of the handle, which serves the dual purpose of locking together the different parts of the weapon while acting as a counter-weight to the blade. 12, 16, 31, 70, 113, 115, 177

Pool.   A tournament term for several fencers assigned to compete against one another. 8, 157, 159

Position.   The placement of the weapon in any of four lines related to the covered target area. Refers to the spatial relationship between the fencer's weapon and the target area. 38–40, 42, 43, 48–50, 59–63, 65, 76, 79, 119, 120, 121

President.   The referee, arbitrator of the bout (replaced by the term "referee"). 21, 116

Pressure.   A lateral blade press on the opponent's blade. 51, 52

Prevost.   A preliminary status of an accredited and licensed fencing teacher or coach before achieving the Master certificate. *See also* Fencing Master. 4, 198

Prime (1st).   A position that protects (covers) the low inside area, thumb toward six o'clock, hand overpronating with weapon point being lower than the hand. 38, 74, 121

Bibliography

Sources, Books, and Magazines

Alaux, Michel. *Modern Fencing: Foil, Épée, and Sabre.* New York, 1975. This contribution to the fencing library was written by the late Michel Alaux, former United States Olympic coach. In addition to a precise discussion of the techniques of foil, saber, and épée, Alaux offers an analysis of most techniques and elements of fencing, highlighting the salient points. Excellent photographs and an interesting account of an eighteenth-century fencing master. An excellent book for all fencers and instructors.

American Fencing (Foster City, Calif.). Published bimonthly by the United States Fencing Association (USFA). The official publication of the USFA, this magazine informs fencers of tournament schedules and results and of rule changes and interpretations. Also includes topics of current interest.

Arkadyev, V. A. *Fencing.* Moscow, 1957.

Barbasetti, L. *The Art of Sabre and the Épée.* New York, 1936. Presents theories and ideas that are quite useful for saber and épée fencing. Reveals the methods of one of the most successful fencing masters—Luigi Barbasetti—of the period.

Bean, M., and G. Gal. *Relazione sullo stage per maestri di sciabola* (Report on the Training Program for Saber Fencing Masters). Budapest, October 3–5, 1986.

Bernhard, Frederica, and Vernon Edwards. *How to Fence.* Dubuque, Iowa, 1956. A loose-leaf book containing eighteen fencing lessons, each of which includes a definition of a specific skill, points to be watched in execution, and exercises to reinforce the skill. Also includes a section on history and one on games and festivities.

Bortolaso, G. *La controffesa, ovvero le uscite in tempo: definizione, considerazioni e confronti nell'ambito dell'evoluzione della scherma moderna* (Counteroffense, the Counterattacks: Definitions, Comments, and Comparisons in the Context of the Evolution of Modern Fencing.) Mestre-Venezia, 1986.

Bower, Muriel, and Torao Mori. *Fencing.* Dubuque, Iowa, 1966. A great deal of information is presented in this seventy-two-page book. Written as a supplement for a beginning fencing class and as a review of fencing history, techniques, rules, and bouting.

Bradford, V., and P. Burchard. "The West German Formula." *American Fencing,* December–February 1989.

Bressan, A. "Considerazioni sulla metodologia didattica e sull'allenamento tecnico-tattico per schermidori di alto livello prosposti dalla scuola di sciabola Ungherese" (Con-

siderations on Teaching Methods and Technical-Tactical Training for Top Fencers). International Saber Clinic, Budapest, "Saber Fencing III," October 3–5, 1982.

Bressan, A., A. De Ambroggi, and L. Di Rosa. *Principi metodologici ed esemplificazioni di una progressione didattica*. (Methodological Principles and Teaching Progressions). F.I.S. Centro Studi Documentazione Ricerche, 1981.

Castello, Hugo, and James Castello. *Fencing*. New York, 1962. Emphasizes the fundamentals of foil fencing "through theory and instruction in fundamental moves . . . practice drills . . . practice bouts . . . and the competitive bout." Especially helpful are the "points to remember" following the presentation of each skill. Of particular interest are sections on conditioning and electrical foil fencing.

Crosnier, Roger. *Fencing with Foil*. London, 1951. Presents a detailed, comprehensive analysis of skills and techniques and explains the tactical situation in which each skill can be used. The competitive fencer will find the sections on fighting and fighting techniques particularly helpful.

———. *Fencing with the Electrical Foil*. New York, 1961. Discusses the effects of electric foil fencing as related to basic movements, the hit, attacks and defense, counter moves, renewals, and presiding.

———. *Know the Game—Fencing*. London, 1952 (Amateur Fencing Association). A comprehensive and compact presentation of the basic skills and equipment required to fence and officiate in foil, épée, and saber.

D'Alessandro, B. "La storia dei campionati del mondo scherma" (History of World Championship Fencing). *Mensile Della F.I.S.,* July, 1982.

D'Asaro, M., and E. G. Kaidanov. *Sabre Training Manual*. Colorado Springs, Colo., USFA, 1987.

De Ambroggi, Alfredo. *Metodi per lo sviluppo delle abilità tecnicodidattiche* (Methods for Developing Technical Training Skills). F.I.S. Centro Studi Documentazione Ricerche, Rome, 1981.

de Beaumont, C. L. *Fencing: Ancient Art and Modern Sport*. New York, 1960. A comprehensive textbook for the modern foil, saber, and épée fencer, whether novice or expert. Includes chapters on tactics, training, judging and presiding, the organization of a fencing club, and the grand salute.

de Beaumont, C. L., and Roger Crosnier, eds. *Fencing Techniques in Pictures*. New York, 1955. Photographs and sketches depicting fencing skills, with concise explanations presented "to confirm instruction received." Each fencing movement is photographed or sketched in four or five phases showing components of the movements. Of the 95 pages, 60 are devoted to foil, the remainder to épée and saber.

de Capriles, M. A., M. R. Garret, and S. S. Sieja. *Tournament Guide for the National Collegiate Fencing Championships*. 2d ed. NFCAA, New York, 1975. A guide to assist host institutions and personnel in organizing major tournaments. Latest edition: See Garret, Corcoran, and Russell.

Deladrier, Clovis. *Modern Fencing*. Annapolis, Md., 1948. Covers the use of the three weapons from a modern or eclectic viewpoint. Of special help to foil fencers is the series of exercises for clubs and organizations that do not have a fencing master.

Di Rosa, L. "Una progressione didattica nella scherma" (Training Progressions in Fencing). Clinic for Fencing Teachers, I.S.E.F., Rome, 1981.

Garret, Maxwell R. *Fencing Instructor's Guide*. Chicago, 1960. To be used in conjunction with or independent of the slide film *Beginning Fencing*, this booklet for the Athletic Institute provides instruction in officiating, scoring, teaching methods, conditioning, and safety.

———. *How to Improve Your Fencing*. Chicago, 1959. By means of photographs and narration, this booklet for the Athletic Institute introduces the beginning fencer to the basic skills of fencing or provides a review of the basic fundamentals for the experienced fencer.

Garret, M. R., Candice Cocoran, and Kathleen Russell. *Tournament Guide for the National Collegiate Fencing Championships.* 3d ed. NCAA. Kansas City, 1980. A guide to assist host institutions and personnel in organizing major tournaments. The authors of the first and second editions were M. A. de Capriles, M. R. Garret, and S. S. Sieja.

Gaugler, W. *Fencing Everyone.* Winston-Salem, N.C., 1987.

Hayden, Rob, and Sheldon Berman. *Introductory Foil: A Manual for Instructors.* Maine Division of the Amateur Fencers League of America, 1978. Available through the national office of the AFLA (now known as the USFA). This manual presents a series of sixteen lesson plans designed for the instructor or high school coach but useful to anyone with considerable fencing experience. An extensive appendix gives additional information on history, basic drills, correcting specific mistakes, footwork, warm-up exercises, infractions and penalties, and club workouts.

Kaidanov, E. G., and J. Glucksman. "Developing Reflex Actions to Respond to Unexpected Situations." *Swordmaster* (NFCAA publication), March 1983.

Klinger, A. K., and M. J. Adrian. "Foil Target Impact Forces During the Fencing Lunge." *Biomechanics* VIII-B, vol. 4B (1983).

Leytman, L. G. *Fencing for Youth.* Moscow, 1961.

Lukovich, Istvan. *Electric Foil Fencing.* Budapest, 1971. Available through fencing equipment companies in the United States. A narrative discussion of the interrelationships of foil fencing components. Blends the old and the new with particular emphasis on the maneuvers and techniques initiated by electric fencing. An appealing book.

Mangiarotti, E. *La Spada* (The Épée). Milano, 1971.

Mezo, F. *The Modern Olympic Games.* Budapest, 1956.

Moody, Dorothy L., and Barbara Hoepner. *Modern Foil Fencing: Fun and Fundamentals.* 1972. (B&D Publications, 6645 Heather Ridge Way, Oakland, CA 94611, 1972. A loose-leaf book geared to the teacher and/or coach. An educationally sound and logically arranged text, well illustrated with stick-figure drawings.

Nadi, Aldo. *On Fencing.* New York, 1943. Nadi is considered one of the greatest fencers of all time. In this book, he shares with all fencers the finest details of his skill. Chapters on competition, infighting, precombat, and combat training are especially fascinating and instructive. Although the book is out of print, it may be in libraries.

The National Association for Girls and Women in Sports Guide: Archery—Fencing. Published bianually by the American Association for Health, Physical Education, and Recreation, Washington, D.C. Approximately thirty-five pages are devoted to fencing. Each issue includes the rules of fencing, brief articles on teaching techniques and organization, and a bibliography.

National Coaching Staff. Report on épée clinic conducted by L. Saychuk at the USFA Olympic Training Camp, Colorado Springs, Colorado, 1989.

———. Report on foil clinic conducted by G. Krystof at the USFA Olympic Training Camp, Colorado Springs, Colorado, 1989.

———. *USFA Foil Manual.* Colorado Springs, Colo., 1988.

Nelson, Marvin. *Winning Fencing.* Chicago, 1975. With brief chapters on épée and saber, this paperback book is a basic source of instruction for both beginners and developing foil fencers. Of special interest is the technical vocabulary appendix.

Palffy-Alpar, Julius. *Sword and Masque*. Philadelphia, 1967. This book clearly describes the skills for épée, foil, and saber. A spirit of discipline and sportsmanship pervades. One of the few books devoted to the history of fencing; training, conditioning, and diet; and the listing of Olympic and World Champions.

Pezza, G. "L'evoluzione della scherma di fioretto negli ultimi 25 anni" (Evolution of Foil Fencing in the Last Twenty-Five Years). Thesis, Italian Academy of Arms, Naples, 1984.

Pignotti, U., and G. Pessina. *Il Fioretto* (The Foil). Roma, 1970.

Roi, G, And A. Fasci. "Indagine sugli eventi traumatici nelle gare giovanili di scherma" (Research on Traumas Suffered by Fencers During Competitions for Young Fencers). Medicina dello Sport, Milan, 1986.

Selberg, Charles A. *Foil*. Reading, Mass., 1976. A comprehensive paperback book for teachers and students alike, with special emphasis on "tactics and the psychological elements of competitive fencing."

Simonian, Charles. *Fencing Fundamentals*. Columbus, Ohio, 1968. A brief discussion of fundamentals. Techniques are covered from the standpoint of definition, use, execution, common faults, and drills.

The Swordmaster. United States Fencing Coaches Association, 37 Griswold Place, Glen Rock, NJ 07452. Official publication of the USFCA, published four times a year. Contains scholarly articles of interest.

Szabo, Laszlo. *Fencing and the Master*. Budapest, 1982. One of the best and most comprehensive books covering such material as basic methods of teaching footwork, bladework, and tactical interaction.

Tyshler, D. A. *Sabre Fencing*. Moscow, 1981.

United States Fencing Association. *Fencing Rules*. Authorized English translation of the rules of the Fédération Internationale d'Escrime. The last edition includes rule changes and additions since 1970. Competitive fencers should have the latest edition. The book includes the general rules of foil, épée, and saber; rules for the organization of competitions; disciplinary rules; NCAA rules; and articles on equipment.

Vince, Joseph. *Fencing*. New York, 1962. For many years Vince taught fencing to Hollywood stars. In this book he shares his experiences in the development of foil, épée, and saber fencers. An explanation of each skill is followed by a discussion of common mistakes and their causes. Considerable emphasis is placed on fencing distance. The suggested fencing drills are excellent.

Volpini, A. *La Spada, Manuale Pratico* (The Épée, Practical Manual). Milan, 1975.

Wyrick, Waneen. *Foil Fencing*. Philadelphia, 1971. Contains descriptions and helpful hints on the nature, value, and purpose of fencing; the purchase and care of equipment; and movement fundamentals.

USFA National Coaching Staff. *Basic Foil Manual of the USFA Coaches College*. Colorado Springs, Colo., 1988.

Visual Media

Annotations for visual media are from *American Fencing* 19 (March 1968), 18, official publication of the Amateur Fencers League of America (now USFA).

Basic Training of Foil Fencing. 16mm black and white sound film made by master fencers and Olympic coaches from Hungary. Excellent presentation of foil fundamental from on-guard position, illustrating advance, lunge, fencing distances, parries, and ripostes. Available by purchase or rental from the University of California, Extension Film Center, 2223 Fulton Street, Berkeley, CA 94720.

Beginning Fencing. 35mm foil film strips in color with accompanying sound records by Professor Maxwell Garret of the Pennsylvania State University. Contains excellent data on offense, defense, strategy, and tactics. Available by purchase or rental from the Athletic Institute, 200 N. Castlewood Drive, North Palm Beach, FL 33408. Also available are related explanatory books, such as *How to Improve Fencing* and *Fencing Instructor's Guide.*

Fencing. A complete series of excellent loop films in standard 8mm and super 8mm, in regular and slow motion with freeze frames. Featured as instructors are Michel Alaux, 1968 United States Olympic Foil Coach, and Csaba Elthes, 1968 U.S. Olympic Saber Coach. Maxwell Garret served as consultant. Fencers demonstrate arm and leg techniques, simple foil attacks, defense, simple attacks on the blade, compound attacks and compound ripostes, individual fencing lessons employing false attacks, and techniques of saber. Available for purchase or rental from the USFA, One Olympic Plaza, Colorado Springs, CO 80909.

Let's Take a Trip. 16mm black and white sound film originally prepared by television personality Sonny Fox. Outstanding film for public information made at the Fencers Club in New York City. Fine presentation of foil, épée, and saber fencing and practice bouts. Available by rental from the USFA, One Olympic Plaza, Colorado Springs, CO 80909.

Modern Fundamentals of Foil Fencing. Portfolio of 16 illustrations covering basic positions, attacks, and parries. 11'' × 14'' black and white, photographed by A. John Geraci. Also in 38mm projection slides. Available by purchase from John Geraci, 279 E. Northfield Road, Livingston, NJ 07039.

NCAA 1980 Foil-Saber-Épée Finals. (Held at the Pennsylvania State University). ½'' or ¾'' color videotape originally prepared by ESPN cable television company of Bristol, Connecticut, for national television presentation in March 1980. Outstanding performances of national college finalists, with descriptive interpretation of actions and rules. A fine educational documentary. Available for rental from the Pennsylvania State University, c/o Emmanuil Kaidanov, 267 Recreation Building, University Park, PA 16802.

Omnibus. 16mm black-and-white sound film originally prepared by the Ford Foundation for television. Outstanding film for general audience presentation to arouse interest in fencing. Excellent cinematography. Available from the USFA, One Olympic Plaza, Colorado Springs, CO 80909.

Technique of Foil Fencing. 16mm black-and-white film featuring Helene Mayer, former world champion, in a presentation of fencing positions and actions. Normal and slow motion with close-ups of hand and foot movements on offense and defense. Available by purchase or rental from the University of California, Extension Film Center, 2223 Fulton Street, Berkeley, CA 94720.

About the Authors

MAXWELL R. GARRET

MAXWELL (MAC) R. GARRET was born in 1917 in New York City. He began his fencing career at Townsend Harris High School under Maestro James Montague and with Maestro Joseph Vince at City College of New York (CCNY). He graduated in 1939 as Captain of the fencing team. In 1940 he began his long career of teaching physical and recreation education and coaching the varsity fencing teams at the University of Illinois (1940–42, 1946–72) and at the Pennsylvania State University (1972–82). At both institutions, he developed numerous Big Ten and national championship teams, as well as many individual champions and All-Americans (son Roger among them). He retired from Penn State in 1982.

From 1942 to 1946, he was commissioned as an officer in the United States Army Air Force and retired as a Major from military service in 1946. During his long and distinguished coaching career, as a Fencing Master in 1960 he was U.S. Assistant Olympic Coach in Rome, Italy; he served in 1969–70 as Head Coach of the Israeli National Team while serving as Director of the Israel Academy for Fencing Teachers. In 1970 he served both as the United States' Head Fencing Coach at the World University Games in Torino, Italy, and as Head Coach for the Israeli National Team at the World Championships in Ankara, Turkey. Mac was one of initiators who instituted the Penn State Open Tournament in 1973, which upon his retirement now bears his name. He served as President of the United States Fencing Coaches Association for three terms: 1950–52, 1960–63, and 1982–84. He served on the U.S. Olympic Committee from 1982 to 1984.

As an internationally ranked fencing official, Mac participates in all levels of competitions. Since 1982 he has continued to be active as a fencing consultant and official. Since 1987 he has been the coordinator for the Senior Age Program (for fencers over forty), which is held annually in conjunction with the U.S. National Championships.

In 1989 Mac and his wife, Diana, moved to Boynton Beach, Florida, where they now reside. Roger, Roberta (1945–85), Esther Garret Solar, Bruce, and their families are their pride and joy. Together they continue to attend and assist at many major fencing events in the United States. In June 1993, Mac and Diana served as members of the Organizing Committee for the U.S. Nationals in Fort Myers, Florida.

EMMANUIL G. KAIDANOV

EMMANUIL G. KAIDANOV is a Fencing Master and Head Coach of the fencing program at the Pennsylvania State University. Kaidanov immigrated in 1979 to the United States from the former Soviet Union, where he had competed as a world-class fencer and served as a coach. He was a candidate for the USSR national team in saber from 1958 to 1964.

Kaidanov graduated from the State College of Physical Education at Kharkov, USSR, where he earned an M.S. in Physical Education with a minor in Anatomy and Physiology and a Master in Sport of Fencing. His post-graduate study includes methods of teaching fencing, research methods, and research on reaction time exercises.

Kaidanov has been a fencing coach for over thirty years and is now in his eleventh year at Penn State. During his tenure, the Penn State fencing teams won two combined national championships (in 1990 and 1991) and finished in the top three every year except Kaidanov's first and third years with the university. Among his students are eight NCAA individual champions and over twenty All-Americans.

Fencing Master Emmanuil Kaidanov is actively involved in fencing education. As a member of the National Coaching Staff, he is one of the authors of *The Saber Course* for the Coaches College. Kaidanov has considerable experience on the international level. Between 1984 and 1992 he coached US teams at the Pan American Championships, World Championships, World University Games, Maccabiah Games, and U.S. Olympic Festivals.

E. G. Kaidanov lives with his wife, Izabella, in State College, Pennsylvania. His son Gregory, who graduated from Penn State with a degree in political science, resides and works in California.

GIL A. PEZZA

GIL A. PEZZA is President of the United States Fencing Coaches Association. He received his diploma of Master of Arms in 1985 from the Italian Academy of Arms in Naples, Italy, with one of the highest scores in the history of the academy.

Pezza began fencing at the age of four under the guidance of Marisa Cerani. During his career as a competitive fencer in Italy, he was coached by Marcello Lodetti, Janos Kevey, and Arturo Volpini. Before coming to the United States in 1977, he had been a member of the Italian National Junior and Senior épée teams and of the prestigious Milanese fencing club La Società del Giardino. In 1977 he joined the Wayne State University fencing team in Detroit, Michigan, where he was coached by Istvan Danosi. While fencing for Wayne State, he was twice NCAA Individual Épée Champion (1980 and 1981). Among his students are three NCAA individual champions and more than nineteen All-Americans.

In 1984 he was appointed Head Fencing Coach at Wayne State. During his tenure from 1984 to 1990, the Tartars men's team captured the NCAA title in 1984 and 1985, and the women's team won team titles in 1988, 1989, and 1990. In 1986 he was appointed to the United States National Coaching Staff, and in 1988 he coached the U.S. women's national épée team.

Pezza holds a bachelor's degree in history and political science, a master's degree in sports administration from Wayne State University, and a Juris Doctor degree, magna cum laude, from the Detroit College of Law. He is a practicing attorney in Detroit, and he lives in Southfield, Michigan, with his wife, Cheryl, and daughter Camilla.